"Off the Strip is every city in the world…"

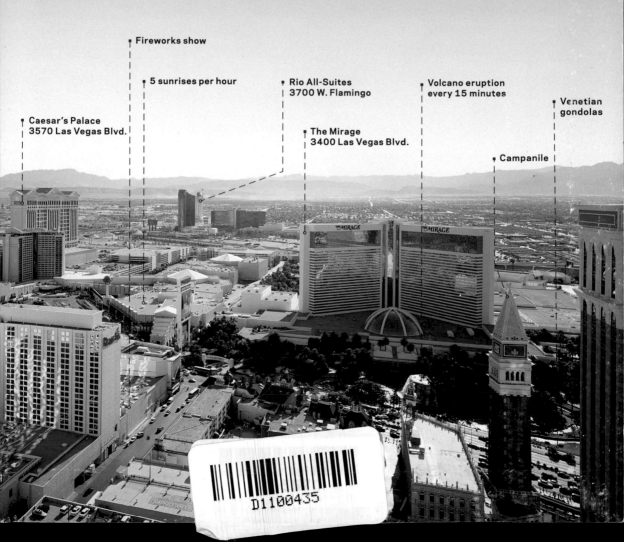

Fireworks show

5 sunrises per hour

Rio All-Suites
3700 W. Flamingo

Volcano eruption
every 15 minutes

Venetian
gondolas

Caesar's Palace
3570 Las Vegas Blvd.

The Mirage
3400 Las Vegas Blvd.

Campanile

university for the **creative arts**

TEMPURA MAHI MAHI

STIR FRIED CHINESE VEGETABLES $8.95 PLUS TAX
AN EGG DROP SOUP

PRIME RIB CR
& SHRIMP BU

	2003	2004
Annual number of visitors to Las Vegas	35,540,126	37,388,781
Economic impact of tourism	32.8 billion USD	33.7 billion USD

	2003	2004
Hotel occupancy rate	89.6%	92.0%
National average hotel occupancy rate	59.1%	61.3%
Average nightly room rate	83.00 USD	90.00 USD
Number of hotel rooms in Las Vegas	130,482	131,503
Average number of nights spent	3.6 nights	3.6 nights

There are over 100,000 weddings in Las Vegas every year.

	2003	2004
Number of convention delegates	5,657,796	5,724,864
Number of yearly conventions	24,463	22,286
Non-gaming economic impact of conventions	6.5 billion USD	6.9 billion USD
Clark County gaming revenue	7.8 billion USD	8.7 billion USD
Las Vegas gambling revenue	6.1 billion USD	6.8 billion USD
Average per trip gambling budget	491.00 USD	545.00 USD

Skyline, New York-New York

Eiffel Tower, The Parisian

75% ORIGINAL SIZE

Pyramids of Giza, Luxor

Campanile, The Venetian

97% ORIGINAL SIZE

Unlike the other themed casino hotels in Las Vegas, in the Venetian original Italian landmarks have been reproduced at almost full scale (between 97-100% of the original). Rather than the wild collage of landmarks juxtaposted at different scales in casinos like the Parisian, the client of the Venetian demanded a high level of historical and architectural accuracy.
The faithful reproduction of the real scale of these iconic buildings and their dense compression on the site generate an effect that is surprisingly urban relative to the other casinos.

The Venetian Resort Hotel Casino
The Stubbins Associates, WATG Inc.

The experience of the Venetian begins at the main entrance, the drop-off for visitors arriving by car from the Strip.

Upon entering, all sense of the desert condition that surrounds the casino – dry, empty, barren, and colorless – is immediately lost. The interior world of the Venetian is temperature-controlled and uniformly lit, a hermetically sealed environment completely independent from the exterior.

mural, c. 16th century

The GrandCanal SHOPPES

EXIT

The 11,150 m² of the ground-floor casino sits on sixty acres of land. 150 Baroque murals by Titian, and Tintoretto and Tiepelo are hung above the thousands of slot machines, blackjack tables, and television screens below.

◆ CASINO ◆

slots, 20th century

Gaming at the Venetian

2,500 slot machines
139 gaming tables
11,150 m² (120,000 ft²) casino space

Total Entertainment → 37 million people visited Las Vegas in 2004. It is a city with 278,700 m² (3 million ft²) of casino space, supplied by 132,000 hotel rooms with an average occupancy rate of 92%. The gaming revenue for a single year was valued at 8.7 billion dollars in 2004; the total visitor dollar contribution reached 33.7 billion.

All rooms at the Venentian are "suites" with a minimum of 65 m² of living space, including a 12 m² bath.

SUITES
23•201
to
23•238

23207
23205
23203
δ 23201

Visitors come to Las Vegas for more than just gambling. The majority of casinos have hotels and convention facilities that attract nearly 6 million delegates annually, a nearly 7 billion dollar economic impact. The Venetian has a total of 4027 hotel suites, with an average area of 65 m² each. Last year the hotel had an annual occupancy rate of 98.3%, with guests paying 219.00 USD per night per suite on average. The Las Vegas Sands Group has recently finished construction of a 1.6 billion dollar expansion project for the Venetian, the "Palazzo Casino and Resort." The new complex adds an additional fifty-story hotel tower with 3025 suites, 9755 m² (105,000 ft²) of new casino space, and 41,800 m² (450,000 ft²) of shopping area.

CHECK
OUT
VENETIAN

The original hotel tower (finished in 2003) has 1013 suites.

"Streetmosphere" → The conditioning of Las Vegas extends beyond material and mechanical systems. To provide a more entertaining experience, brimming with references to both the real and imagined Venice, the Venetian features a daily spectacular where singers and musicians perform in the "streets" of the second floor Grand Canal. A new, hybrid atmosphere where Verdi fuses seamlessly with high-end shopping, accompanied by the sounds of an electronic keyboard.

Artisti dell'Arte → "These entertainers are classically trained singers and actors from all over the world. Come and enjoy several unique shows as these talented performers take you back in time to Renaissance Venice. Performances begin in St. Mark's Square at 11:30a.m. and continue throughout the day until 8:30 p.m."
www.venetian.com

Las Vegas Venetian Library →
Contained within this twentieth
century replica is "Madame
Tussaud's Celebrity Encounter",
a museum filled with figures of
celebrity replicas created in wax.

Verdi, La Traviata   **Sony**, electronic keyboard

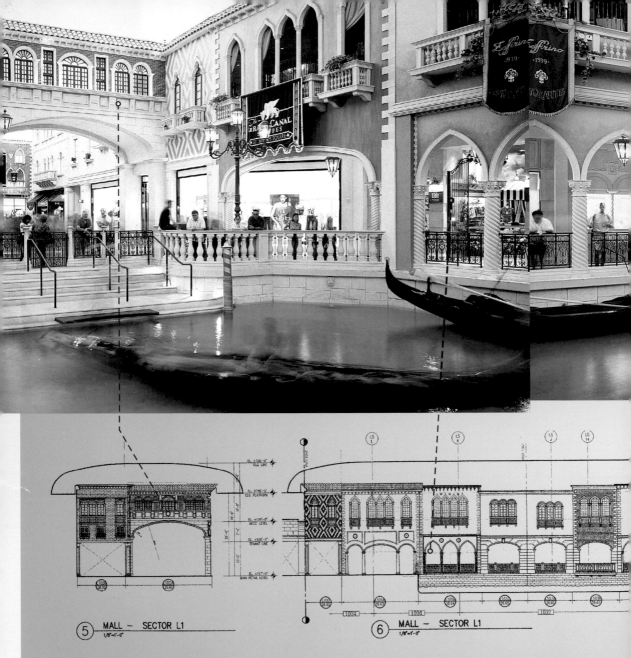

(5) MALL — SECTOR L1
1/8"=1'-0"

(6) MALL — SECTOR L1
1/8"=1'-0"

Grand Canal Shoppes → Visitors can stroll down a bustling Venetian street at dusk, complete with canal (with blue water, unlike the original version), gondolas with singing gondoliers, wandering minstrel singers, stores, restaurants and speciality food shops. On an average day, 35,000 people visit the Grand Canal.

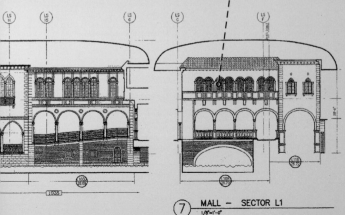

(7) MALL — SECTOR L1
1/8"=1'-0"

Fasten your seat belts! → Although the canal in the Venetian is only 0.5 m deep, visitors use the seat belts provided for extra safety. This is the kind of "scripted space" described by Norman Klein (→ page 35), a Venice that is "abbreviated, accessible and always air-conditioned." A space of Architainment: a recognizable copy of Venice that is new and squeaky clean, where the ease and comfort of the copy exceeds that of the original.

In this version of Venice, the gondoliers moonlight as opera singers. As they sing, their voices are transmitted throughout the shopping area via wireless microphones.

The research for The Venetian began with a one-week trip to Venice. Architects from The Stubbins Associates recorded their sensations of the city and sketched building facades, impressions which would later be translated into the design of the casino. In the Canal Shoppes the architects have included all the kinks and bends of the real city – there are no long vistas, and pedestrian bridges have been deployed to further break the space up into smaller individual "neighborhoods."

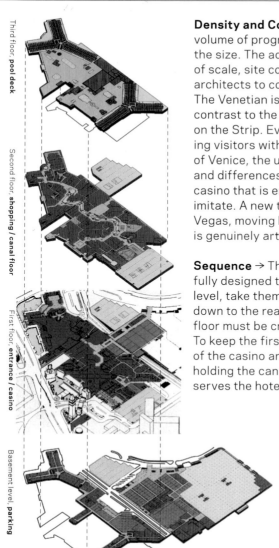

Third floor, **pool deck**

Second floor, **shopping / canal floor**

First floor, **entrance / casino**

Basement level, **parking**

Density and Compression → Although the Venetian has the same volume of program as the Bellagio, it occupies only one third of the size. The added demands of historical accuracy, preservation of scale, site conditions and local zoning requirements forced the architects to compress the program on the site. The result is that The Venetian is much denser and more urban than its neighbors, in contrast to the automobile-based experience more commonly found on the Strip. Even though the Venetian project was intent on providing visitors with an exact replica or 3-D snapshot of the original city of Venice, the unique site pressures, technological advancements, and differences in programmatic requirements have produced a casino that is entirely different from the Venice it was intended to imitate. A new type of urban space within the desert expanse of Las Vegas, moving beyond reproduction to produce an environment that is genuinely artificial, a new form of authenticity.

Sequence → The circulation sequences of the Venetian are carefully designed to draw people up into the second floor shopping level, take them to the end of the retail sequence, then bring them down to the rear of the first level casino so that the entire gaming floor must be crossed in order to exit the building.
To keep the first floor empty for the open, non-partitioned spaces of the casino area, the second and third floors are much denser, holding the canal shops and the twelve pools of the roof deck that serves the hotel towers above.

◄ To preserve the sensation of being under a real sky, the vaulted ceiling over the Canal Shoppes is designed to have a continuous curvature without any seams or lighting hot-spots. To maintain the illusion, the architects painted hundreds of exposed sprinkler heads in various hues of blue and white. During installation, the color of each sprinkler head was picked to match its location underneath the hand-painted sky mural.

13

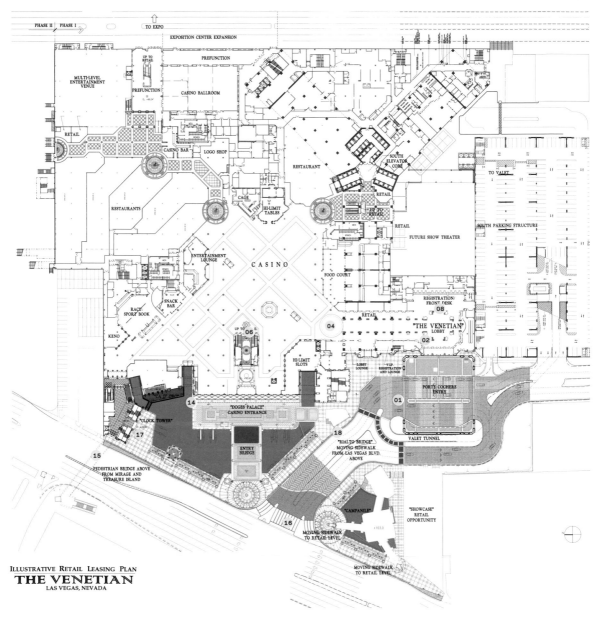

ILLUSTRATIVE RETAIL LEASING PLAN
THE VENETIAN
LAS VEGAS, NEVADA

First floor plan

According to a casino architect, a typical team of people working to complete such a building might include up to 400-500 consultants working on the design side of a project, and up to 2000 individuals working with the contractor. These consultants vary from project to project, but generally include: structural engineer, mechanical engineer, electrical engineer, civil engineer, landscape architect, lighting consultant, signage graphics designer, food service provider, security, surveillance, theater consultant, life safety, and ADA (disabilities) compliance.

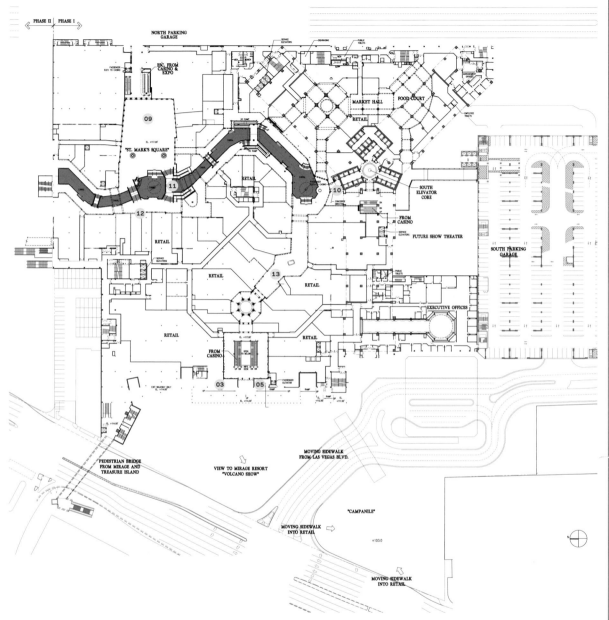

Second floor plan

The interior facades are drywall construction with add-on pieces designed by The Stubbins Associates. The variety of building types and interior facades comes from the recycling and repetition of these add-ons in a variety of colors, stucco patterns and weathering finishes. This "kit of parts" consisted of hundreds of unique pieces, catalogued and documented in nearly four thousand construction drawings.

Materials → In upper areas of the facade that do not experience a lot of wear and tear, the architects have taken more material liberties, substituting real stone with a pressure-injected foam material coated in weatherproof paint.

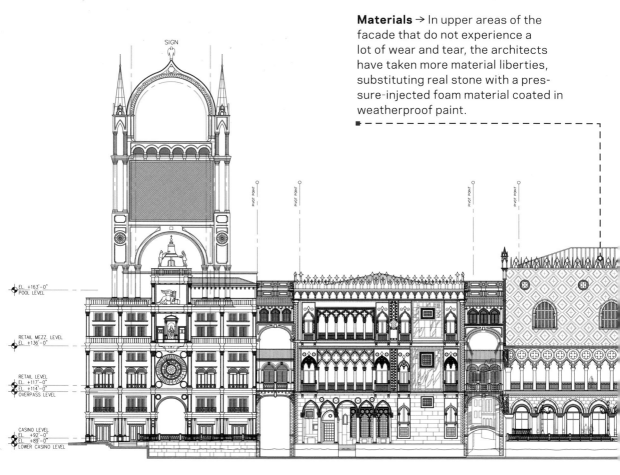

SIGN

EL. +163'-0"
POOL LEVEL

RETAIL MEZZ. LEVEL
EL. +136'-0"

RETAIL LEVEL
EL. +117'-0"
EL. +114'-0"
OVERPASS LEVEL

CASINO LEVEL
EL. +92'-0"
EL. +89'-0"
LOWER CASINO LEVEL

PIVOT POINT

CLOCK TOWER   CA' D'ORO BRIDGE   CA' D'ORO   DOGGIAS BRIDGE
NICHE 1   NICHE 2

Unlike the original, the Vegas version is ADA (Americans with Disabilities Act) compliant.

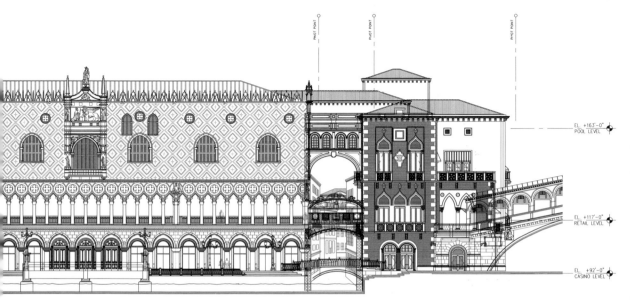

EL. +163'-0"
POOL LEVEL

EL. +117'-0"
RETAIL LEVEL

EL. +92'-0"
CASINO LEVEL

DOGES PALACE

BRIDGE OF SIGHS
PONTE DELLA PAGLIA
NICHE 3

PALAZZO CONTARINI FASAN

THE
VENETIAN
3355

Abridged and condensed → In this reproduction of Venice "with a twist," the major tourist destinations of the real city have been compressed into a single experience. The Rialto bridge, the Doge's Palace, and the Ca d'Oro are placed in a continuous sequence, watched over by the Campanile (reproduced at nearly full scale) that sets the Venetian apart from the Eiffel Tower, the Statue of Liberty and the other vertical landmarks that define the Strip.

Ca d'Oro

17

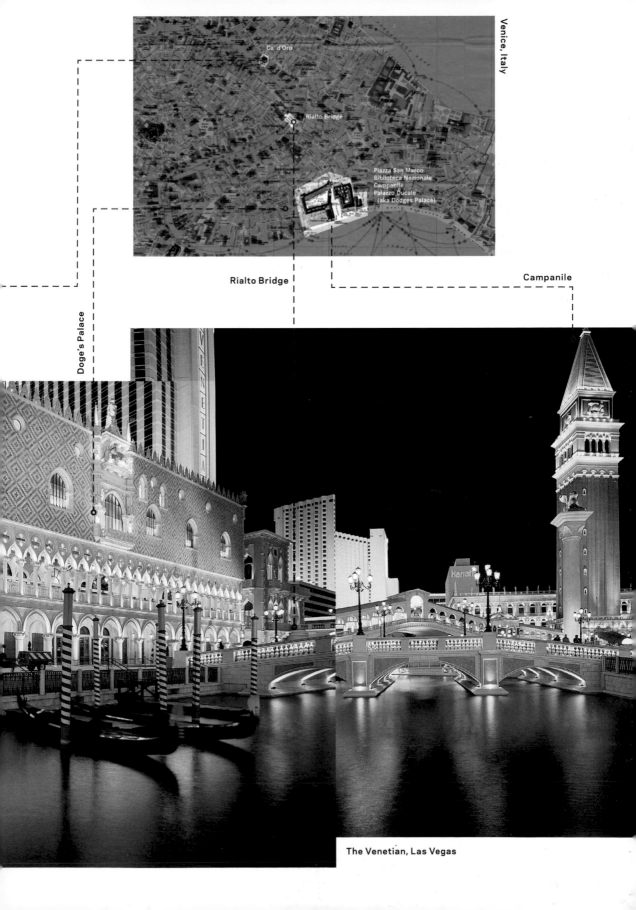

Venice, Italy

Ca' d'Oro

Rialto Bridge

Piazza San Marco
Biblioteca Nazionale
Campanile
Palazzo Ducale
(aka Dodges Palace)

Doge's Palace

Rialto Bridge

Campanile

The Venetian, Las Vegas

At night, the Strip becomes one large stage set. Brilliantly illuminated, the texture of the city transforms from a haze of concrete and blue sky into a shimmer of neon lights and glowing surfaces.

data **Venetian Casino Resort →** Location: Las Vegas, NV. **Client:** Las Vegas Sands, Inc. **Designer/Architect:** A collaboration between TSA of Nevada, LLP (The Stubbins Associates) and WATG Inc., of Nevada. **Structural engineer:** John A. Martin Associates; Martin & Peltyn. **Mechanical engineer:** AE Associates; MSA Engineering. **Construction period:** April 1997 – August 1999. **Site Area:** 25 hectares (64 acres). **Floor area:** 557,400 m² (6 million gross ft²). **Number of floors:** 36. **Structure:** Steel and cast-in-place concrete. **Maximum height:** 122 m (400 ft). **Interior design:** Wilson & Associates; Dougall Design. **Photographs:** Ramon Prat.

verb Norman Klein is a writer and theorist of thematized commercial environments like Las Vegas. The spectacle in the middle of the desert is a paradigm of what Klein calls the Electronic Baroque, the equivalent in the information age of the illusionistic architectures of the 17th and 18th centuries. Governed by an extreme hybridization of public space with commerce, the new scripted spaces of the Electronic Baroque are far larger in scale and more pervasive in their effects than the fantasy environments of the past. Government, illusion, and commerce all bleed together to create a new space where Las Vegas, shopping malls, and the election of George Bush become different manifestations of the same phenomena.

The Electronic Baroque:
Las Vegas, the mall and George Bush

Extracts from a conversation with Norman Klein

Glossary

Scripted Space
a walk-through or click-through
environment (a mall, a church,
a casino, a theme park,
a computer game), designed to
emphasize the viewer's journey
– the space between – rather
than the gimmicks on the wall.
This type of space allows the
viewer/user to enter and feel
as though he has limitless
options, even though the reality
of the space is one of extreme
precision engineered for a
specific purpose or "mode of
seeing." This might be equated
to something like a "fabricated
freedom."

Artifice
lavish, immersive fakery.

Las Vegas Architainment
(late 20th century) cities are
abbreviated, accessible, and
ALWAYS air-conditioned. This
type of controlled environment is an instantly recognizable copy; the safe version
(especially post-9/11) where
the charm of the artificial
exceeds the real/original.
These replicas – New York,
Paris, Monte Carlo, Venice,
Rio – are condensed versions
of their real selves, yet appear
large through the precise use
of *trompe l'oeil*, forced perspective, and carefully staged
multiple vanishing points.

In Las Vegas, Artifice is a primary system for scripted space
and immersion. The architectural entertainments inside and
around the casinos on Las Vegas Boulevard (formerly the
Strip) offer a contract for the visitor. One freely decides to
"most likely" lose money gambling, but in return is given
a few hours of aristocratic power; a fake aristocratic power
of course, but this is artifice on behalf of entertainment.
Here entertainment is the papacy.

We then leave Vegas, slightly lighter, modestly in debt.
Any of a hundred cities today somehow seem to have
parallel grammars to Vegas' architainment. And indeed,
the outer skin of the Canals of Amsterdam, or New York's
Times Square seem to share that dizzying use of Artifice
as advanced tourism. There are also differences, of course.
Once we leave the boulevards, the gaudiness of stately,
illusionistic streets, we find neighborhoods (quartiers,
barrios). Here the uniqueness is easier to understand.
These micro-climates are the heart of the city and is how
we study the difference between Vegas (illusion) and other
cities. We relinquish the 150 year fascination with great
entertainment boulevards and enter the world of infrastructure, urban governance, ethnic complexity, and so on.
Indeed, comparing the boulevards to the neighborhoods has
become one of my central tools when teaching this material.
I notice that today many students have a profound fascination with industrial cities (having vanished in Europe and the
US essentially), with a world that seems more authentic,
a world of lofts and weathered brick. But that too is an illusion. The process of collective forgetting and noir imaginar-
ies is not so different from the illusions of "the Strip."
Historical examples also fit into this discourse. To give
you a sense of the discourse that emerged around the
entire Baroque grammar of special effects and "scripted
spaces" – for example, in the painting of ceilings and domes
– remember that Michelangelo was criticized for painting

too much like a sculptor. As late as 1765 in the engravings of his Sistine Chapel, by the younger Pannini, the twisted figures are depicted as sculpture, as *trompe l'oeil* paintings. The fascination with logarithmic solid geometry and with quadrature (the squaring of the round) led to complicated debates about who possessed the correct solidity and paradox in their painted ceilings and domes. One might say that the merging of sculpture with accelerated and ironic perspectives turned into a navigable illusion very similar to the movies themselves – by the mid-seventeenth century (even with Kircher's magic lanterns, as a commentary on frozen sculptural animated effects).

Clearly, Michelangelo was not fundamentally interested in perspectival *trompe l'oeil* (not as much as other artists of the period), but he understood precisely what was being asked: to blend sculpture with the flat surface, to make a neo-Platonic statement about the strange way that God manifested Himself in the eyes of "man."

My research indicates that two problems around this dynamic about ceilings and domes repeat themselves. One is immersion: to remove the foreground from the space and privilege the viewer, giving the illusion, at least, of free will within a scripted space. The second is the strange narrative that goes best with this kind of architectural illusion – almost always an epic tale about relinquishing one's freedom on behalf of a greater power, the appearance of choice, but in fact the ritual surrender of power to the authority (the program, the pope, the state).

There is also a third point of reference that is almost never absent during the centuries of special effects staging of space: the contested ironies between machine-made illusion and "nature." I put the word nature in quotes because it was a highly problematic code here. For the Baroque, nature (what appears natural to our eyes) had to be invaded by Artifice (inspired by the mind of God). Thus, the more artificial (as one stayed longer inside the space), the more ontologically pure and more a pilgrimage, into the handmade of God's image, becomes a metonym about reaching that which can never be truly represented and only understood as a heavenly absence – the ultimate nature, the mind of God.

However, immersion can also diminish the power of Artifice, as it is meant to do in nineteenth-century panoramas and dioramas. Here, the longer one stayed, the less one could distinguish between handmade irony (illusion), and the sense of nature (winds, sky, natural light, etc.). Thus there exist two

Painted Ceilings / Domes (18th century) domes and vaulted ceilings like the Sistine Chapel employed complex representational techniques to manipulate the viewer's perception of space. Through technologies of image-making like perspective foreshortening, *trompe l'oeil*, and quadrature, architects transformed enclosed spaces into expansive immersive environments that seem to shift and move around us. Though their effects were fantastical, the science behind their choreography was carefully researched and precise (using rules of perspective coupled with the curvature of the vaulted ceilings and domes).

Trompe l'oeil (18th century) an illusionistic style of painting in which objects are depicted with photographically realistic detail.

Panorama (19th century) attractions that were 360 degree wrap-around views of that staged various scenes, historical and current, from around the world. (i.e. the Battle of Gettysburg, bazaars of Jerusalem, or views of along the length of the Mississippi river). A panorama in Regent's Park, London, attracted over half a million visitors in one year alone. Sometimes the visit to a panorama was even better than the real thing: buildings were always viewed in sharp focus, nothing was ever closed for repairs, views were never obscured by foul weather or smog... Usually contained in large, warehouse-like structures, these panoramas were "scripted to give the illusion of open space." Machine and nature became interchangeable. A Chinese visitor visiting the London Panorama noted, "Only when one reaches out to touch [the panorama] does one realize that it is just a wall, just a painting, just an illusion."

Electronic Baroque (1955-present) Klein defines the Baroque as a scripted space where the distinction between public and private is difficult to establish. After the Renaissance, Baroque techniques such as painted domes were used as a tool of political and social stabilization. Today, the Electronic Baroque is characterized by a similar blurring between public and private realms, but advances in techonology and the growth of neo-mercantilist power have made these new scripted spaces far more potent and powerful, governed by a hybridization of public space with commerce.

vast traditions of immersion – one from the Baroque, and another from the industrializing nineteenth century.

The first privileges artifice as power; the second conquers (or seems to replace) nature through machine-made illusion. We take these messages into the local cineplex today, to watch a special-effects blockbuster. Clearly, both Artifice and the panoramic coexist here. Indeed, our Electronic Baroque era has merged the new traditions of special effects. It is rather like blending the industrial collage with the CG morph, to be both endless and as intimate as the card trick of a master magician.

One can proceed into architectural examples by the hundreds and begin to understand how immersion, scripted spaces, Artifice, and the panoramic are merged in seemingly countless formulas, each slightly different. Unfortunately, the merging of the two, under the overwhelming visual authority of entertainment, has removed the very sense of paradox that allowed these systems to evolve into new forms and grammars.

Indeed, our civilization has recovered aspects of the Baroque system of special effects – the use of Artifice, the obsession with Scripted Spaces as an instrument of power. Our software vaguely echoes the Baroque use of perspective. The parallels are extraordinary and perhaps the most frightening of these is political. The Baroque was marked by intense instability within the so-called Early Modern State. Part of this instability was created by the awkward alliances set up by monarchs to remain in power – negotiating with the merchants of the bourgeois class in order to form an uneasy alliance with "natural" enemies (i.e. the French and English revolutions). Thus, Baroque illusions reflect aspects of this uneasy alliance (mercantile illusions on behalf of scripted spaces defending the power of the monarch).

Today we see alliances between a flattering national government and global media, who represent the very antithesis of the old-fashioned national state. We also see fundamentalist religious wars similar to those of the seventeenth century, an instructive parallel reminding us that our civilization has left the Enlightenment, and is evolving new forms of autocratic government; another example of "make it new," but one that is perversely dangerous.

Then there are the machines of illusion themselves. In the seventeenth and eighteenth centuries, machines were often turned into miniaturized illusions, called "toys," that were not for children but rather for glamorous display, a part of the occult identity of machine in the Baroque era (or eras).

Certainly the industrial transformation extracted the toy from the machine, but regarding computers, I wonder if both the Baroque occult fascination with technology and the industrial cult of the machine have met. I am currently studying how industrial technology transformed into collective "forgetting" (or misremembering) and how the twentieth century was imagined before this transformation ocurred. It seems that the relationship between technology and the collective imaginary is dominated by narratives about how power steals or represses personal identity.

I am utterly convinced that media, collective forgetting and illusion are part of a political grammar that has afflicted our culture more than enriched it, but can lead to extraordinarily rich directions over the next few decades. Technology tends to respond to economic uncertainties, both as an imaginary and economic tool. To follow the uneasiness of an era (how it manifests economically and socially) reveals why one technology is more successful than another. There are so many potential directions left unexplored and effective technologies that have been ignored. There is no Spencerian logic here.

The best technology does not necessarily win, only the machine that eases social unease and strengthens the power of the emerging system of governance. People love to be governed by a machine that takes away modernity, that removes uncertainties. People complain, revolt, but in the end, the system of power has defined identity.

Of course, the writer's job, like that of the artist, is to humanize alienation and to show how machines are not simply enemies or friends, but are in fact our fondest desire and our worst nightmare convening inside the same mechanism. Thus, there is a profound link between the cult of technology (i.e. science fiction, positivism) and the illusionistic scripted space. They both promise endless potential at a cost that the viewer pays all too willingly. The machine stands in for the God we want as a servant, but who will we accept as our monarch.

verb

Sit down. Relax. Turn on your home theatre. The lights start to dim as the A/V system kicks into gear. To understand where Verb will take you on this journey, all you have to do is put the first Star Wars movie into your DVD player. Yes, the one from 1977. Now, compare it with the latest, from 2005. Between one and the other, the information age has intervened. Watch the story, the characters, the actions, the movements. Look at the architecture too. The imaginary cities of 1977 and those of the latest installment... Don't you get the feeling that everything has become much more complex? More baroque? What was promoted twenty years ago as an audiovisual marvel now seems like an almost intimate work of children's theatre. And, of course, thus was the myth born. What today is a spectacular and marvelous sensory illusion. In the current movie, what is fascinating is the inability to separate the real from the digital, because they already form part of the same nature.

The Baroque too was, after the innocence and searching of the classical Renaissance utopia, a twisting of forms and a sensory illusion. To compare:
— The Renaissance is to the modern industrial era what the baroque is to the information age.
— Brunelleschi is to the 15th century what Le Corbusier is to the 20th.
— Rome is the Las Vegas of the 16th century.

After the modern renaissance comes the electronic baroque. The *e-baroque*.

Verb Conditioning resumes the journey to a real nowhere by means of a world of fascinating, thematized architectures. In the era of the electronic, the border between the real and the invented begins to be as diffuse as in the movies. Architectures conceived as recreation, like a second nature. Designed for enjoyment, consumption and fashion, constructed narratives in the form of a tropical landscape or the canals of Venice. Where the background music always plays, the light comes from an artificial sun, the breeze is always pleasant and the temperature is always perfect. Now turn off the DVD. Turn up the lights in the room a little and let the music play. With the remote, gently put your seatback in the upright position. Verb wishes you a pleasant trip...

Neuschwanstein
Excalibur

Excalibur Las Vegas, re-envisioned in the Bavarian Forest. Image courtesy of Graftlab.

Promotional brochure that reproduces a spread from the June 1962 issue of ARCHITECTURAL RECORD. This material has been brought to our attention by Alex Wall, author of a book on Victor Gruen whose preparation has partially coincided with the production of this issue.

DESIGN FOR A BETTER OUTDOORS INDOORS

Victor Gruen, architect of the Cherry Hill shopping center, says of the design concept, "The underlying purpose of the enclosed mall is to make people feel that they are outdoors—to provide psychological as well as visual contrast and relief from indoor shops —yet at the same time they are provided with the comfort of air conditioning, the chance to sit down and rest a while, and the visual enjoyment of landscaping, fountains, and sculpture." The concept has been skillfully carried out at Cherry Hill, as the photo at left will reveal.

This large center—two department stores, a supermarket, and 75 shops—focuses on a concourse 1,370-ft long, in an L shape, which terminates in three courts, the largest of which, photo at left, adjoins the Strawbridge & Clothier department store. This space, called Cherry Court, is 110 by 172 ft in size, and rises through upward sweeping curves to a skylight 46 ft above the floor. Daylight also reaches this area from clerestory windows in the two side walls. In addition to the fountain, this area includes a Japanese garden, complete with arching bridge and running water, and a fanciful wood gazebo where one may sit and relax.

Joseph W. Molitor photos

Cherry Hill Shopping Center
Delaware Township, N. J.
PROJECT ARCHITECTS: *Victor Gruen Associates*
ASSOCIATE ARCHITECTS: *Strawbridge & Clothier Store,*
George M. Ewing Co.
INTERIORS: *Strawbridge & Clothier Store, Welton Becket;*
Food Fair, Kasoff & Bifano;
Cherry Hill Cinema, William Riseman Associates
LANDSCAPE ARCHITECTS: *Lewis J. Clarke*
CONSULTANTS: *Traffic, Wilbur Smith & Associates;*
Real Estate, Larry Smith & Co.

Verb Conditioning

Effects

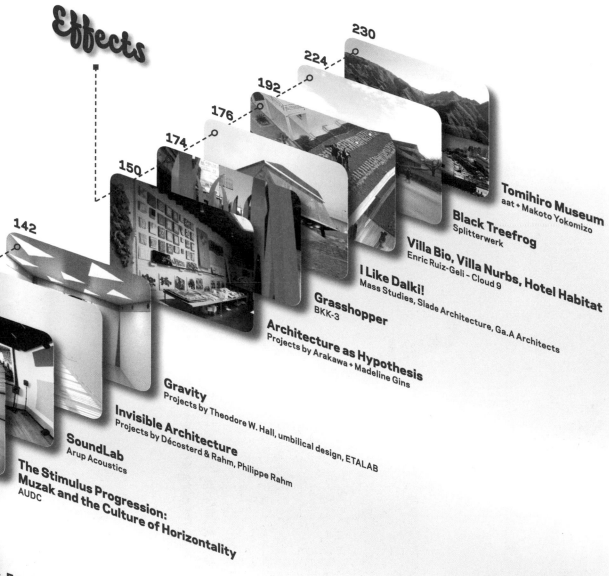

verb The fourth issue of Verb looks at two related processes: the conditioning of architectural environments and the conditioning of behaviors. On the one hand, studies of luminosity, sound, atmosphere and temperature expand the range of techniques available to the discipline, allowing the production of ever more extensive effects with increasingly minimal means. On the other, the rise of commerce, theming and the manufacturing of identity produce a different set of effects, directing users and their emotions for maximum commercial success. What are the real potentials of conditioning? Do these new environments merely replicate the existing with increasing accuracy and sophistication, or can they generate qualitatively new atmospheres capable of stimulating not just new effects but new forms of living? In the end, the difference between environments and behaviors is not so easy to distinguish.

verb

17°C

If the e-baroque is the defining condition of the digital age, it is no surprise that architects look directly to the Baroque itself for inspiration. Unlike Norman Klein, Gagat International is interested in the formal potentials of Baroque ornament, deciphering their geometric logics and proliferating them into new forms. The geometrical complexity of the Baroque merges with the modeling capabilities of advanced computer software to produce hybrid forms of contemporary ornament.

Rococo Relevance

Luc Merx, Christian Holl - Gagat International

'Rococo Relevance' is an attempt to reactivate the history of architecture as a reference for contemporary architecture, at a time when the computer opens up new possibilities in the generation of virtual worlds. If one examines the computer's influence on contemporary architecture, one is left disappointed by the results that have so far emerged from these possibilities. For one thing, this discourse has been restricted to a small group of intellectual pioneers who focus on unvarying references that include biological and scientific metaphors such as self-similarities. It seems that the computer does not influence our work directly, but only circuitously, via the work of a few colleagues. Little remains of the freedom that the computer seemed to proclaim at the start of the 1990s. This freedom was kept in check by voluntary self-restraint and the exhilaration activated by the forms of complex geometrical structures, which failed to question the image of the building and its functions and never fully exploited the potentials of virtuality. Concerning its foundations and expected reception, digital architecture remains closely attached to the patterns of modernism, and its production adopts the character of manifestos. In such a reduced reception of classical modernism, these manifestos are illustrations of principles that deprive us of all sense of doubly curved surfaces, complex geometries, and the integration of the image into architecture. The virtual nature of the computer invites us to succumb to illusions about the quality of the constructed architecture, our control over the execution, and makes us forget how dirty, rough and banal architecture really is.

Similarly, history is also misused as a retouched image. Beyond the possible ironies of postmodernism, retrogressive initiatives become fixated on the reproduction of one period, but fail to assimilate the quoted architecture. Retro-architecture is formal, opportunistic and dogmatic. It is reactionary. It is negatively founded as anti-modern and as anti-avant garde. Its achievement is at best to make history a topic of consideration once again.

Rococo Relevance moves between aversion and fascination. Rococo Relevance studies the instilled rejection of the formal, of the figurative, of the unjustifiable and of the non-Euclidian. Rococo Relevance concerns itself with ornament and simulation, with effect, instead of believing in an inherent truth that needs to be revealed.

What distinguishes our work from the usual practice of the art historian is radical subjectivity. History is examined for its architectural applicability and for the possibility of adopting a position in relation to the potentials of the computer and virtuality. We are uninterested in artistic intentions, unless we can make use of the artist's work as a driving force for our own production. Rococo Relevance breaks with a taboo. The aversion that we observe within ourselves is important precisely because we wish to avoid what it evokes. Rococo Relevance is an attempt at liberation. Not only does the aversion to ornament drive us, but also the aversion to the figurative, to the atmosphere; the aversion to the unjustifiable, to intuition. Rococo Relevance combats the acquired dogma of abstraction and of honest construction.

The architecture of the late Baroque is pervaded by *inganno*, the play of illusion and simulation. Under the influence of Andrea Pozzo, vaulting was endowed with architectural illusions until well into the late 18th century. Images merged with real architecture, no longer separated from its surroundings by a frame. The focus of illusionary painting is the transition from the virtual to the real. Even though these images are static, their effect is dynamic in the sense that it interacts with the viewer's movement. The frescoes play with the ambivalence that arises when one is caught succumbing to an illusion, as the visual reading of the vaulting flickers between an understanding of the existent construction and that of the extended space of illusory architecture.

Pillars made of *stucco lustro* imitate marble and are applied in layers, only a few millimetres thick, simulating the typical veining of composite marble. As in computer rendering, the spatial structure of a material is suggested by means of a wallpaper-like definition of a surface. *Stucco lustro* was very popular for precisely this reason: It allowed a greater level of control than was possible with real marble – the form and

colour of the veining could be exactly planned. Though more expensive than marble, *stucco lustro*, the simulation, was given priority over the original.

The efficiency of the image, which determined the choice of material, also determined spatial planning. Architecture had a front and a back, but similar to theatre, the hidden was only hinted at and the rear was missing. Thus, resources were concentrated in the visible parts of the space. The economy of this manner of thinking corresponds to rendering, where the work of depiction is likewise concentrated on the visible area: the unrendered rear of a wall is neglected, practically non-existent. To actually design it is a waste of time.

Above and beyond rendering, the late Baroque period also anticipated the radical geometrical changes effected by computer-aided design. The baroque vaultings of Balthasar Neumann and of the Dientzenhofer family do not achieve the degree of complexity foreseeable using today's tools. However, their effect eclipses the digitally generated architecture of recent years.

Another important element in Baroque architecture is the *rocaille*, which is significant not only as ornament, but also as an architectural utopia. Here there is no difference between floor, wall and ceiling; the surfaces form convex and concave curvatures. Often, rocaille is not static, but depicts a frozen moment in a dynamic process. It creates hybrid spaces, in which furniture and architecture are intertwined with each other and with nature.

The Augsburg ornamental engravings suggest how rocaille may be viewed separately from its scale. Beyond its actual significance, ornamentation gains importance as a spatial, architectural model. Conversely, rocaille's lack of scale can foster a new understanding of the ornamental. Just as ornamentation serves as a model for architecture, so can architecture become ornamental on a smaller scale. The parallels between the lack of scale in rocaille and in CAD programmes are significant.

Experiments → While the theoretical section of Rococo Relevance focuses primarily on the 18th century, the experimental segment of our research addresses our relationship to the computer and present-day production methods. Through prototypes and installations, we are trying to understand how tools influence their products: how they facilitate or complicate certain aspects of production and influence the decision-making process.

The growing similarity between the present-day and the 18th century can be traced, among other things, to technological innovation. Rococo Relevance is an attempt to condense this non-articulated influence, to make predictions about this process, and to direct the development of future projects. This development can be influenced through the conscious selection of production tools. For example, the use of the computer programme Maya has facilitated the design of complex forms, and has made orthogonal design more difficult.

When contemporary techniques differ from those of its antecedents, the examination of historic parallels may enable one to recognise and exploit the potentials of the new tools. Beyond the direct influence of the new instruments, one should

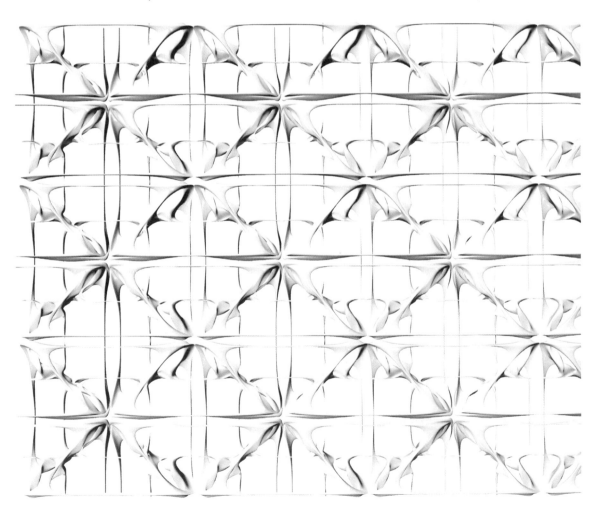

not neglect the extent to which thinking – and design – is indirectly influenced by the repetition of certain activities. Thinking in terms of surfaces, which characterises the work of rendering programmes, inevitably affects our view of space.
The significance of perception increases. Textures and the visual qualities of materials supersede the primacy of construction and implementation.
Part of our research examines these two-dimensional patterns. At first, their creation (the definition of surface via a wallpaper-like appliqué) only serves the realism of the image. However, the architect must also deal with symmetry, repetition, similarity and variation. If she or he understands these principles, the production of a genuine wallpaper is but a small step. In the rendering process the white wall loses its obviousness. Rendering opens up one's eyes to the alternative, to wallpaper.
Computers and printers have expedited the production process of wallpaper design, simultaneously simplifying repetition and the production of unique patterns.
The design process of custom-made, unique wallpaper surfaces implies the exact matching of scale and proportions to a space. The patterns can react to the periphery, the centre and the corners of the wallpaper.

The same problems arise in the case of relief and the production of three-dimensional structures. Here too, the computer makes the initial design work easier, regardless of whether it is a unique specimen or a repetitive structure, and issues of rapport come to dominate in the process of implementation. In these spatial structures, the production of prototypes requires more work than the production of wallpaper. With the aid of a CNC milling cutter, computer data is transformed into actual models. Taking small steps, we attempt to re-create the formal control of 18th century designs. The white wall, which was made colorful and ornamental by wallpaper, is again called into question by means of reliefs. The surface is distorted. Using rhythm, repetition and similarity we try to organise the plethora of ornamentation so as to avoid a restless effect.

An intermediate form of wallpaper and relief are the rendered images of three-dimensional structures. These illusionist images can be printed and applied like wallpaper, offering greater material and formal freedom than mill-cut ornamentation. Based on spatial models that reflect the actual light conditions of their destined locations, these three dimensional designs are interesting images that remain unbuilt, given the current limitations of the CNC milling cutter. These altered reliefs are an attempt to transcend the frame, the division between image and reality, and correspond to the peripheral area of Baroque frescoes.

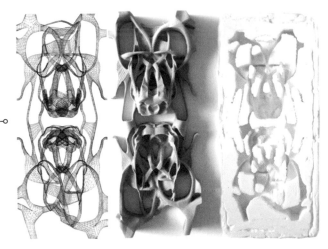 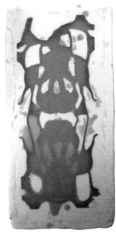 

In 1996, before the start of the Rococo Relevance project, material imitations of the 18th century had already led to an installation as part of the Vergessenprojekt ('Forget Project'). In this installation we (Luc Merx, Anne-Julchen Bernhardt and Verena Merx) tried to reactivate the efficiency of the Baroque notion of material. During one night, the installation re-created a world consisting solely of surfaces. Funder, a wood-construction firm and contractor, produced a type of chipboard with imitation palisander laminated on one side. The result was a world of wallpaper that resembled that of rendering. Architecture becomes an image that one can enter. Regardless of the standpoint of the viewer, the image may function or else collapse. The installation creates spaces that achieve the perfection found in renderings and at other points reveales the means through which the illusion of perfection has been achieved. It is a condensing of the location; it is not a replacement for an existing situation, but rather an overlay. As in Baroque frescoes, illusion and reality exist simultaneously. Rococo Relevance builds upon the Vergessenprojekt's concept of reality: it is fragmentary. At present we tend to create problems rather than solve them, insinuating more opportunities than we are able to take advantage of.

The project is not meant to promote studies on the late Baroque. It is instead an attempt to define the history of architecture as an instrument for the development of a personal architecture. The addition of the rococo to familar references underscores the amount of potential lost through incestuous discussion and the convenient persistence to adhere to old lines of thought. Rococo Relevance is the new architecture of old Europe.

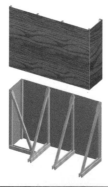

The e-Baroque arrives in Würzburg...

Gartensaal 05
Gagat International

Baroque space is more than the play of illusion and virtuality. The Gartensaal 05 installation confronts the geometry of space, reflecting Balthasar Neumann's vaulting and the spatial concept of rocaille. The Gartensaal is especially suited for an experimental study of the late Baroque. In this 'Garden Hall' Neumann applied many of the principles that he employed in ecclesiastical architecture to this secular building. The pillars are layered with stucco lustro and while in the ceiling fresco the illusion is of secondary importance, the insertion of the image into this space is an example of the typical integration of the virtual into Baroque architecture. The parallels between Neumann's vaulting and the possibilities of designing doubly curved surfaces with the aid of a computer is evident and often mentioned in architectural discourse.

Ledges and other elements of purely architectural decoration merge with the plaster cherubs and floral ornamentation. Small mirrors emphasise the skin-like quality of the unpainted areas of the vaulted ceiling and mark a transition to the ceiling fresco mediated by the magnificent rocailles of Antonio Bossi.

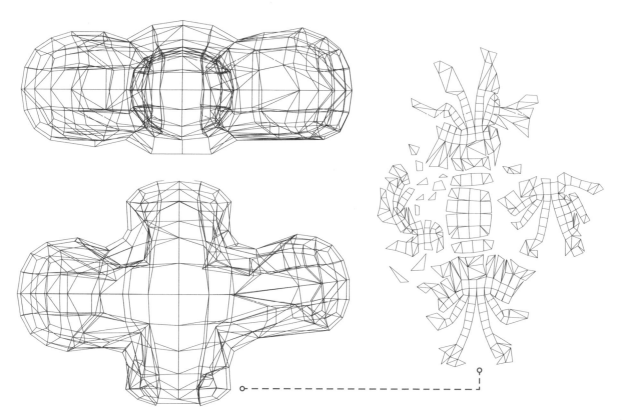

The installation used an inflatable structure that was quickly and easily assembled, safe and economic, and adaptable to the scale of the Gartensaal. The installation would have been impossible without the help of a computer, though parts of the design were completed without its use. The main aim was the resultant object and not not the purity of the process. A sewing machine, our own level of handicraft skills, and the limitations of the fabric contributed as much to the final form as did the computer.

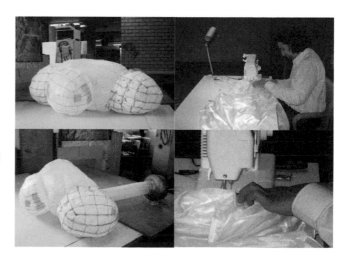

Quite early on we decided that although the installation would be developed for the Gartens aal, it should also be shown in other places. Thus the piece had to function in the Gartensaal, i.e. in a context which is quite specific and unlike almost any other, but also as an autonomous object, independent of location.

The basic form is of five interlocking and interconnected cells – one large, elongated middle cell and four smaller adjoining ones. Each cell displays a different pattern and vary slighty in size and arrangement. They are similar but not identical.

The installation has a double wall and the patterns of the inner and outer skin are the same. The double skin forms an air chamber and create an interior walk-in cavity. The object is inflated by means of four ventilators with a pressure valve controlling the rhythmic pulsation of the installation. This rhythm changes according to interior movements.

The lower part of the object is made of airbag fabric. To withstand contact with the floor, this fabric had to be robust and washable, and light enough to allow for easy inflation. Parachute fabric, which is lighter and more transparent than airbag fabric, was used in the upper areas. As this part of the installation is less likely to become dirty, a more sensitive material could be used.

The outer form of the installation is relatively distinct and is derived as a negative form of Neumann's vaulting, which is a series of interpenetrating cone-shaped segments that are often distorted.

On the interior the basic form is hardly recognisable. The space is furrowed and fragmented, moving and changing far more than the outer form. There is no difference between the floor, the wall and the ceiling; it is a simplified variation of the rocaille space of the Augsburg engravings, which show that rocaille was not only intended as ornamentation, but also as an architectural model and as a spatial utopia. The existence of these engravings make Bossi's stucco work and that of his contemporaries especially significant for present-day architecture, suggesting parallels to the computer-aided design of contemporary spatial models.

data

Rococo Relevance → Gagat International, Luc Merx in collaboration with: Technische Universität Kaiserslautern, Stefan Rinnebach, Torsten Bodschwinna, Holmer Schleyerbach, Christian Holl. **Installation Gartensaal 05** → In collaboration with Core: Alexander Buchop, Holger Grobe, Petra Langer, Holger Leibmann, Sascha Querbach, Marcellus Schwarz, TU Darmstadt. **Photographs:** Peer Cassebaum, Stefan Schneider, Gagat International. **www.gagat.com**

Structured Ornament: Experiments with Blank Typologies

Studio at Harvard Graduate School of Design, Spring 2005
Farshid Moussavi

Contemporary building technologies, the need for totally controlled environments not subject to the contingencies of natural cycles or the urban environment, and an increasing trend to densify city centres are all contributing to a growth in the size and number of typologies that require a blank envelope: shopping centres, department stores, cinemas, museums, libraries, concert halls...

These types require not only an envelope that separates interior and exterior, but also bigger service voids, plants, retail areas, storage, and server rooms. In the process, the demands on the skin of the building have evolved from the regulation of environmental conditions and the relation to urban life to a new set of requirements that range from branding to contextualising, from hiding to revealing. Their scale is incongruous with existing urban fabrics, and this poses certain questions about the capacity of architecture to integrate them effectively.

In this context, a relevant investigation is the introduction of ornamentation and décor in the architecture of these blank buildings as an organizing device, associated simultaneously to the cultural and urban realm as well as to issues of internal structure, function and cladding. This studio explored ornamentation as an operative device to organize blank typologies in order to integrate them within the urban realm or to represent their content, questioning the depth of the envelope beyond its purely technical and functional requirements to become a filter between internal functions and external constraints. As a problem that we have often faced in our practice at FOA and for which there is not sufficient theoretical background, the research is motivated by the lack of an effective theory of ornamentation that can be used to address this very contemporary problem. The correlation between the inside and the outside of buildings can be framed historically, from Roman poché space to the Baroque search for variety and theatrical effects beyond building functions, to the 19th century debate between Semper and Loos on ornament. While for Semper the functional and structural requirements of a building were to be subordinated to larger semiotic and artistic goals through ornament and the visual delimitation of space, in Loos's view, ornament was used in traditional societies as a means of differentiation; since modern man needed not to emphasize his individuality but to suppress it, ornament had lost its social function and was unnecessary.

The International Style and post-war modernism brought to architecture the obsession with transparency as a device of architectural "sincerity," as opposed to the more bourgeois habits of décor. Architecture was no longer supposed to disguise functions but to make them visible, to render the city and its buildings immediately readable. This concept determined the material qualities of the façade, as a layer that was designed to disappear and expose building functions. A critique of this approach was promoted in the 1970's by architects like Venturi and Scott Brown, who denounced the modernist paradigm as cynical and inefficient, proposing ornament as a more operative device than transparency for integrating buildings within the urban realm and to communicate with the public. In this model, ornament accepts a radical detachment between buildings as function and buildings as representation, treating the contradiction between systems of space, structure, program and representation as a positive factor. With the demise of postmodernism, Venturi and Scott Brown's return to décor and representation has been abandoned as a legitimate approach to architecture. But in the contemporary situation, both the older transparency paradigm of functionalism and the idea of "Light Construction" that has pervaded contemporary debate lack effective devices to address the requirements of these ever-expanding blank typologies.

Ornament as necessary or contingent →
The inability of theorists to agree on even basic terms with regard to ornament illustrates the difficulty in deciding which of a building's functions are in fact primary. Ornament has been typically opposed to function, structure and necessity, but in biology there are numerous examples where

the integrity and survival of a species depends on ornament. For example, Darwin describes the peacock as all ornament. In terms of fitness for survival, however, the size of the peacock's tail is a huge impediment; sexually it is very attractive, so their breed is incredibly successful at reproducing. Equally ambiguous is the distinction between *core form* and *art form*, originally made by 19th century theorists like John Ruskin, Viollet-Le-Duc and Otto Wagner. In the case of painting, for example, there is an inherent ambiguity in the nature and necessity of the frame: the frame serves to limit the field of the painting and give meaning to its body, but the frame does not by itself carry meaning. Again, it is impossible to break down what is essential and what is accidental: both are dependent.

Ornament as deep or superficial → Façades can have primary visual functions, which can be either deeply connected to the core form or a superficial pattern independent from the core form. But they can also be both physically superficial and key to the function of the organism.

The best example of superficial ornament comes not from architecture but from the camouflage of war ships during the First World War. Here, quasi-Cubist patterns on the hull made it difficult to determine from a distance the shape, size or direction of the ships. A more radical case is the F-117 Stealth bomber, an example of perceptive function affecting the core structural form. The need to design the body of the plane so that radar cannot detect it has resulted in a plane that defies its perception effectively, but its unusual geometry makes it very difficult to fly.

Ornament as opaque or transparent → Is ornament deployed to "decorate" the content of a building, or is it a device to project an entirely different content over the container? Loos adopted a vision of the modern metropolis as an arena where the individual is almost crushed by forced intimacy and the repressive powers of the social-technological mechanisms of a mechanical *Gesellschaft*. To survive, one has to escape identification. Unlike traditional ornament – such as tattoo in "primitive" cultures – modern clothing becomes an anti-sign or non-transparent sign, the function

of which is to disguise its referent – to mislead. In Loos's buildings, the façade, like clothing, also assumes the role of masking: in his houses, there is a radical disparity between the interior and the exterior. Again, these categories have come into dispute: recently there has been a rebirth of tattooing in Europe and America, as an expression of identity and sexual daring.

Ornament as contextual or representational → Is surface ornament related to the broadcasting, branding or representation of a content (physical or symbolic) intrinsic to the object, or is it derived from the environment where it needs to be placed? Ornament can be a contextual mask over the core function of the building – as in Peter Eisenman's Columbus convention centre, where the exterior skin is derived from generative urban grids to provide a scale to the street façade removed from programmatic references to the interior – or a transparent filter over the core function, as in Jean Nouvel's Cartier Foundation in Paris or Toyo Ito's Tower of Winds in Yokohama.

Ornament as meaning or construction (product or process) → Is ornament connected to communication and representative functions, or to the embellishment of the process of assemblage and construction of the object? Is ornament related to meaning (determined by a final state or performance that is determined *a priori*) or to material organization (connected to a process of assembly or growth)? For example, Loos advocated a system of appearances in which a new material would look distinct from any traditional material through an ornamental enhancement of its natural properties. The ornamental nature of the material interventions implicit in quarrying, slicing, polishing and mounting stone to achieve these effects requires precise artistic calculation.

The studio used a current commercial development in Leeds, UK as our field of research, focusing on each of its four programs: a galleria, a John Lewis department store, a cinema and a car park. What follows is a conversation about the problems and potentials of ornament, based on the student projects that were developed over the semester.

Structured Ornament: Experiments with Blank Typologies. Studio at Harvard University Graduate School of Design, Spring 2005 → Professor: Farshid Moussavi. **Teaching assistant:** Michael Kubo. **Students:** Chad Burke, Joseph Chartouni, V.W. Fowlkes, Fred Holt, James Khamsi, Rick Lam, Mark Lawrence, Shannon Loew, Yekta Pakdaman-Hamedani, Brian Price, Emory Smith, Elizabeth Stoel, Jessica Yin. **Visiting critics:** Hanif Kara, Friedrich Ludewig. **Final review participants:** Eric Carlson, Michael Cesarz, Scott Cohen, Jon Emery, Kenneth Frampton, Toshiko Mori, Farshid Moussavi, Sarah Whiting, Ron Witte. **Material from Farshid Moussavi's studio course "Structured Ornament, Experiments with Blank Typologies" (Spring 2005) used with permission from the Harvard University Graduate School of Design.**

Department store James Khamsi

The John Lewis stores have not typically exploited the possibility of the building envelope as an extension of company's identity, despite their situation in both urban and suburban contexts throughout Great Britain. The project reinterprets John Lewis' cooperative corporate structure as a structural and visual relationship between part and whole, by devising a base increment that is then aggregated to form the envelope. The pattern developed through the increment resonates with the striped logo of the John Lewis brand, using the stripe to create effects of phenomenal depth, phenomenal transparency and phenomenal slowing. The effects of the envelope are developed in response to both the varying conditions of speed and vision that exist on the site, and the demands of the various programs of the department store interior, using tartan-like effects to superimpose these registrations. Site conditions are registered through a series of diagonal corrugations on the façade that express the stripe in light and shade, while interior conditions are registered through vertical and horizontal bands of opac-

James Khamsi

ity, translucency or transparency. In contrast to the strategies towards commercial architecture initially forwarded by Denise Scott Brown and Robert Venturi in the 1960's, which engaged the commercial through the use of legible significa-tion, this project aims to achieve visual reso-nance through the use of non-symbolic effects.

ERIC CARLSON *The project is about making new kinds of relationships that are different from what has typically been done in these kinds of architectural environments. In retail, we have*

James Khamsi

James Khamsi

to build quickly, and so we know certain things before we know other things. We know the exterior before we know the interior, and this project tries to deal with that through the façade alone, which becomes the opportunity to make certain kinds of connections to the environment and to how people move around the building versus people in cars. That's extremely important in determining how the building is perceived. Here the branding is applied onto the building directly through architecture – there's no signage – which has a huge potential.

SARAH WHITING The rippling of the skin is extremely interesting to work with in terms of the differences in perception of people moving at different speeds. Right now, however, the triangle of the diagonal cut at the entrance and the triangles of green windows read more strongly than the stripes, almost as if the stripes alone were seen as being too banal or too Venturi-esque (a.k.a. pure signage). Just playing with the stripes and the bend of the façade might actually have given the façade everything it needed.

FARSHID MOUSSAVI The project is an interesting test of ornamentation being at once contextual and representational. This is done through the envelope of the retail box, which is pixelated through a diagonal aggregate that resonates with the department store brand and differentiates through the incorporation of differing perceptual pressures and exterior functions surrounding the envelope. The differentiated envelope should ideally lead to a diversification of the retail model: just as the building reacts to its context, so the interior layout should provide a unique experience. The existence of multi-channel shopping means that shopping

in a physical environment has to move away from simple scaled variations of the same 'selling model' to spaces of difference, closer to the experience of going to a ride, to a movie... The differential ingress of natural light and views through the envelope then become opportunities for the retail diagram to proliferate into a unique specimen for Leeds.

....

Department store Emory Smith

As artifice and industrialization have compromised the role of ornament as an external display of quality and wealth, commercial developments have been required to employ more sublimated modes of decoration. The spectacle of shopping itself becomes the primary attraction; relationships of building to object, building to subject, subject to object, and subject to subject become the new media of the spectacle. It is within these relationships that the proposed retail skin asserts its ornamentation, as a means of engaging experience, rather than as a conveyor of messages. The skin becomes a visual modulator of context, crowds and content, branding the spectacle itself.

The façade is comprised of a triple-layered glass system of three coordinated patterns that aggregate or separate through perspective to provide opacity at specific viewpoints and transparency at others. In contrast to these fixed viewpoints, a condition of depthlessness and ambiguity predominates as the subject moves around the building. This unpredictable spectacle becomes a field for the emergence of both order and content, focus and fetish.

FM *This project manages to take a glass curtain wall beyond a device of 'sincerity' – of exposing the interior – to co-develop with its environment. The potential of the envelope is a new, ornate materiality where the borders between the physical and the programmatic material are imperceptible.*

SW *It successfully demonstrates how the play of transparency, display cases, and views into the interior work in concert at the level of a boutique. The simple idea of augmenting the display case to the scale of the whole building is intriguing. The whole is slightly mute but very animated nonetheless, and it results in a describable and identifiable box (or brand) for the store. I wonder* how the accumulation of these elements appears as one is driving by, when the building is seen as a façade rather than as an object.

EC *To design in terms of vibrancy, to design something that's animated and engaging is a good way to attract people. But testing is important, because there needs to be a critical level of activity to activate the façade and provide that allure. The Prada building in Tokyo is a five-story, all-glass box on a very small-scale pedestrian street, which very few people walk down; fewer manage to get inside, and even fewer manage to reach the upper levels. So people walking by see that the building is empty, and therefore not vibrant, not fashionable, and not commercial.*

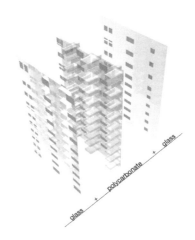

SW *While the Prada Tokyo store is figural from far away and entirely abstract as one moves closer, this project moves from abstraction to abstraction. The pattern is astonishingly beautiful, but it would be helpful to get a sense of how the façade operates at the scale of the full building, the middle scale, and, finally, the scale of the boutique.*

RON WITTE *The project is like a beehive in its relationship of the unit to the totality: a close view reveals unique kinds of activity whereas from a distance you see the vibrating totality of the whole mass. I wonder if it will look like just a box when you put it into context (rather than a resonant box). It may be too subtle to achieve the full scale of urban resonance that this huge building requires.*

· ·

Department store Jessica Yin

Department stores typically rely upon relatively rigid guidelines – department depths, turning angles for aisles, programming of walls and columns – that optimize the shopping experience for maximum consumer purchases. These issues of consumer behavior exert pressures on the shopping floor, which has led to the adoption of two typical systems, often working in combination with each other. On the one hand, a standard column grid permits flexibility, but without additional cladding it cannot easily provide the necessary surface area for display. On the other hand, partition walls are rarely structural and isolate departments too definitively from each other. This project uses a structural system of "net-walls" to mediate between wall and columnar systems, preventing both the redundancy of a columnar grid and the proscription of the wall system.

The structural system is a diagonal grid that deforms in strategic locations to make larger openings for functions such as passage and display. The structural parti consists of a wrapper around the outside of the department store and concentric rings of the net-wall on the interior. The structural elements, panelized in order to facilitate fabrication of the structural pattern, have a "crimp" element (for stiffness in bending) and a "flange" element (to provide attachment for glazing assemblies and provide opacity). By varying the three controls – deformation, crimp size and flange width – the net-wall can accommodate enclosure, opening, light or display, and variations between wall and column on the interior.

KENNETH FRAMPTON *The structural concept for the façade is derived from the spanning grid of the floors, which is then transferred into a load-bearing network along the perimeter. This connection between the grid-like spanning system and the grid-like, but non-orthogonal, wall system is then altered to meet a different criteria, of complexity and permeability. The elevations suggest that these big forms might gain an added value through a rhythmic quality. There are places in the lower elevation that acquire this rhythmic dimension through a forest-like, wind-blown effect, but these effects stop at the upper levels because of the play of empirical requirements behind the façade.*

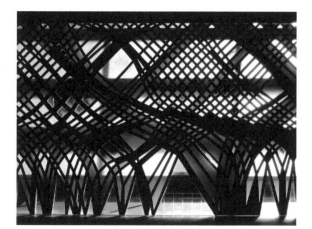

Jessica Yin

SW *On the south and west façades there is a rhythmic differentiation from bottom to top which is functional, in that it's more open on the ground level. The lower level is quite designed, whereas the upper level relies only on the stair core for that differentiation.*

FM *The project explores construction as a system of ornamentation over 'meaning.' Rather than communicating interior functions, it focuses on material organization and the virtuality of the process of production. It uses discrete functional elements such as stair cores, shop windows and entrances to the department store as excuses to introduce differentiation within a mesh structure that creates an enclosure for the retail box. Performative redundancy here creates a structure of ornamentation that goes beyond questions of rigor and economy to questions of vigor and robustness. The system grows inside the retail box to organize not only performances relating to the urban space, but also those relating to the retail layout.*

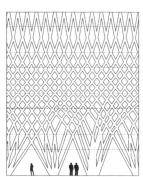
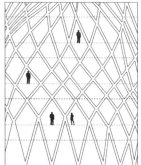

Exterior

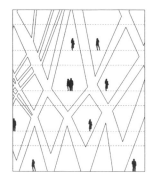

Interior

Jessica Yin

....

Department store Elizabeth Stoel

In department stores, buyers of goods learned new roles for themselves, apprehended themselves as consumers, something different from the mere users of goods. Thus, the department store stood as a prime urban artifice of the age, a place of learning as well as buying: a pedagogy of modernity.
–Alan Trachtenberg, *The Incorporation of America*

During its first 100 years, the department store played a defining cultural role: it instructed consumers about dress, home decoration, and life in the emerging consumer culture of the twentieth century. Today, the social relevance of the department store is dwindling. The traditional department store is losing market share to retailers on both ends of the consumer spectrum – to big-box discount stores that exist outside the city, and to the higher-end fashion stores that cater to the wealthy. For the traditional department store to continue to flourish it must reinvent itself, to become a far more porous and accessible object within the urban realm.

This project uses a system of undulating vertical strips to generate both a legible "blank box" icon for John Lewis and an interactive surface that opens as one moves around it, splitting apart to reveal display windows, entrances, and large, cantilevered lounge spaces. The undulations respond to programmatic and environmental needs, providing seating, views out to the city, and diffuse lighting for selling areas. In its relationship of ornament to effect, the project reflects the attitude that an effect operating solely sensually may inspire a one-time visit, but will not transform visitors into repeat customers. The project marries the desire for initial effect with the functionalist notion of the exterior as a reflection of interior program, deepening the skin to allow program itself to become ornament. The various modes of inhabitation put pressure on the skin, causing it to bend and split and becoming its decorative motifs. Nevertheless, there is a looseness to these relationships: a desire for the visual effect of continuity causes curvatures within proximity to programmatic

Elizabeth Stoel

demands to respond in a ripple effect. The visual and the functional thus operate side-by-side, giving way to the usable, the occupiable – perhaps even the pleasant.

KF *In the relation of the department store to the public, it's always risky to propose that some of the store spaces could become activity spaces, although it is an interesting legacy of the department store type. If one could achieve the right kind of hybrid – and this is also applicable to buildings outside the urban core – one could create a commercial unit with more complex amenities that could feed off of one another to a certain extent. The large bulges that accommodate sitting areas and other types of public program lead this very interesting façade almost to the point of caricature, because it's so exaggerated in its undulations.*
FM *This line of investigation demonstrates the potential for hybridity or composite materiality*

as new possibility for ornamentation. There are lots of examples of hybridisation surrounding us – where a department store is also a museum – as in the case of Selfridges in London with their shows on Bodycraze, Tokyo, Vegas, Brazil... This project is interesting because it goes beyond the laying of one function on top of the other. It is not only a functional and structural hybridisation, but explores hybrid materiality. The envelope is composed of a new material aggregate that mixes the cladding system with the display system and the system of natural lighting, as well as event spaces.
RW *It would be interesting to load the thick condition of the façade with parameters such as aisle widths and widths of display units, or to reflect the syncopation of structural demands like decking or slab dimensions. The perspectives are entirely convincing as depictions of how these spaces – this wall – would foster relationships between the inside and the outside.*

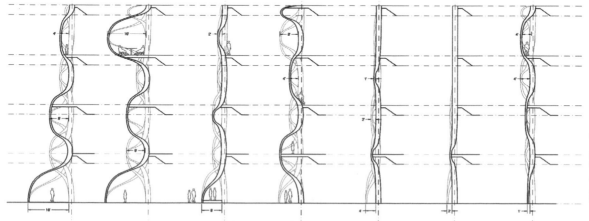

Elizabeth Stoel

Department store   Chad Burke

A study into the effects of natural lighting on the retail environment established a set of performative criteria for the department store envelope, using ornamentation as a device to navigate between the deep functions of the skin and their thin or superficial effects. The skin reacts and twists to exterior conditions to produce the specific indirect lighting levels required by the different interior programs. A reference to the historic textile industry in Leeds is used as a metaphor, reading the woven structure of the skin as a way of contextualizing a national department store brand in a specific regional location. These two primary operations of the skin overlap to create a system of patterning that is both complex and ambiguous.

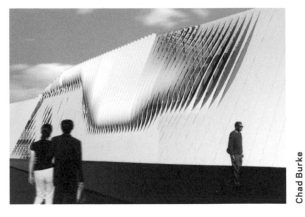

Chad Burke

FM *The project is interesting in that it exploits the possibilities of a purely technical requirement – shading – as a system of ornamentation that destabilizes the simple hierarchies between structure and ornament. The gradual shifts in orientation of the louvers against the ground plane produce a number of perceptual effects that distort the reading of the volume. To extend the functions of the envelope beyond a sun device, one needs to be more deliberate about the effects to be produced with the system. For example, it's great that looking at the perspectives we think the wall is tilting. The opportunity here is that a technical system serving 'core' functions is able to produce unexpected effects within the exterior realm.*

SCOTT COHEN *It would turn the tectonics of the project into a ground for the production of*

scenography. It's a certain kind of visual mirage, a production of effects that are not directed toward anything having to do with the building functions themselves.

FM *These blank buildings present a great opportunity for experimentation. There is an increasing demand on them to be 'unique' while economical means are tight and their content alone presents the urban realm with blank skins devoid of any interest. Here is an opportunity to explore the technical and economical world within which they operate for spatial and architectural effects.*

KF *The project also potentially answers the question of how ornament and structure can be synthesized. This synthesis depends on the potentials of a relationship between a cultural artifact and nature, in the play of sun and weather on the façade. It also uses the variation of the envelope based on the demands of structure and the sun to articulate a very large building, by using the changing conditions around it to overcome the hugeness of the object.*

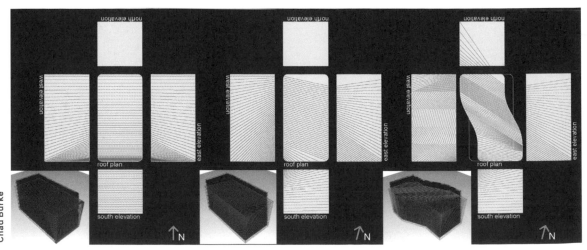

Chad Burke

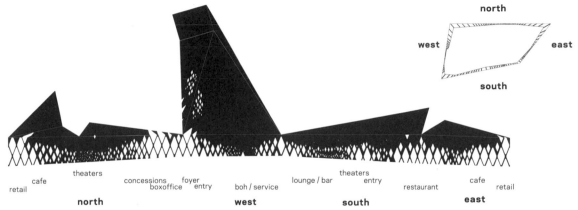

north
west   east
south

retail   cafe   theaters   concessions   foyer   boh / service   lounge / bar   theaters   restaurant   cafe   retail
                     boxoffice   entry   entry

north   **west**   **south**   **east**

Fred Holt

Cinema   Fred Holt

In suburban contexts, simple decorative *appliqué* has traditionally been used to dress blank typologies, turning them into architectural billboards that advertise their function through icons and pastiche. In contrast, ornament is an embellishment of the necessary, a design technique that resolves issues specific to program while providing visual and cultural connections with the urban environment. In urban contexts where the relationship to adjacent buildings and the user determines the vibrancy of a given program, the architect must pursue a design methodology which places the city's needs and the client's desires into a symbiotic relationship. To exploit the urban condition of Leeds, the visual and physical permeability of the building envelope and its adjacencies become the generator for evolving the skin from a blank typology, which screens its activities, into an agent of specificity. The porosity of the skin is contingent on both functional needs and urban adjacencies and vantage points, varying from a thin, perforated concrete bearing wall, to a deep structural lattice that can be inhabited by ancillary program while blurring the threshold between interior and exterior. The result is a building that maintains a strong visual identity within the city while opening the cinema's public amenities – café, restaurant, and concessions – to the constant flux of urban activities around the building.

RW *One of the most important elements here is the relationship between program and surface. In this project the surface is configured in gradient terms. I wonder about the relationship between program – which gravitates towards specificity and exactitude (theaters "need" to be* blacked out in order to show movies and public spaces "need" to be transparent) – and our frequent insistence on a gradient relationship to wrap these distinct zones. Here the gradient is achieved by placing the demanding programs – the theaters themselves – in the center so that other more gradient-tolerant programs can be wrapped around them.

FM *This project is an interesting case of the envelope devoted to both 'decorating' the content of the building and to revealing some of the programmatic content within. In this way its system of ornamentation is both opaque and transparent. This shift between hiding and revealing the interior produces an intricate mask, a differentiated lattice, with radical scale shifts across its extent that avoid the monotony of a cladding system across such a large surface.*

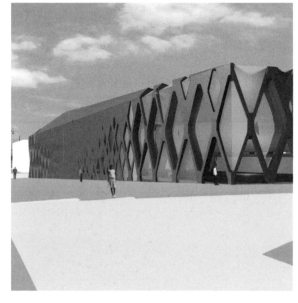

Fred Holt

Galleria Brian Price

This proposal for a contemporary ornament arises from the typological distinction between the model of the Parisian arcade and the modern department store. While the former condenses a street into a building, the latter detaches the building from the city, creating an object-island. An intermediate model could be the kaleidoscope, which creates an abstract sequencing of the singular image behind the apparatus, an image that is both single and multiple. Like a cellularized field of signs, the kaleidoscopic is concerned with producing effects through the multiplication and patterning of a single image.

On the Leeds site, the unit stores of the galleria form a narrow corridor whose axis terminates

signage, collapsing the conventional storefront into a model of oblique signage. By adjusting the depth-to-width ratio, the oblique storefront is able to increase display space while preventing glare on the oblique glazing. Each cell modulates the surface-image of the galleria interior: changing with the orientation of the viewer, the cell reflects the image of the store interior when seen frontally, or permits direct viewing of the interior when seen obliquely.

SC *An important relationship for the consumer is the desire for both a certain kind of differentiation, and a certain kind of connection with others. This project subjugates the individuality of the stores to the totality to an extreme degree. The question of identity and differentiation*

Brian Price

at the anchor department store, the result of a financial diagram in which the anchor store motivates the movement of shoppers through the unit stores. The department store is thus intended to be seen frontally, as an object-brand, while the retail units of the galleria are seen in the oblique as one moves towards the anchor store. The project uses the dependence and contradiction of these two programs – the galleria and the department store – to develop a skin which performs differently when seen frontally from a distance and when seen in the oblique. The face of the conventional galleria storefront is rotated to generate an oblique cell which functions as both direct retail display and

would have to reemerge, likely at the scale of the bands themselves, in order to contend with those who would beg for that level of differentiation at the scale of the individual stores.

EC *Some other projects have tried to give an identity to the exterior skin of the department store, where there is only one brand. Here we're in a galleria, which is almost the inverse, and the project achieves nearly the same level of homogeneity with a point of departure that is commercial, the study of display and visibility. This debate exists within the world of shopping centers: In Hong Kong, shopping centers try to achieve a strong identity through white walls and glass façades, where the indvidual store* signage always has to be put behind the glass. In 90 percent of the other shopping centers around the world, the stores all want their own four meters of façade with exclusive signage, lighting and logo – everyone fights for their own Disneyland identity to make themselves noticeable. This project responds in a very classical architectural way, by declaring that the overall identity of the galleria is more important than the identity of the individual stores.

SC This is a different model of shopping. It's more like shopping in a Tokyo electronics district, where one thinks less of the individual merchant, but where those merchants are encountered in a very direct, intimate way. For this project to involve that kind of intimate encounter there would have to be a completely different interface with the products at the lowest level, at the ground.

KF In the traditional arcade, the farthest architecture went towards the oblique was the bay window. Another issue with arcades is that, because their origin is pre-department store, they have functioned heavily on a prestige basis, where the floor and the roof of the arcade are all part of the prestige of the space. Those arcades that have never lost their prestige are charged with that sense of wealth, but this project is about something much more popular. In the perspectives, there is a very strong sympathy between the roof and the façade of the galleria in terms of material and geometry, but also a departure. It is completely seductive. But if one tries to read the images, the diamond of the walls and the roof may actually pull too quickly – the kaleidoscopic effect drives you forward, and you might miss the stores.

RW In all of these spaces the stores themselves are bypassed. The difference between an arcade and a mall is that one passes through an arcade on the way specifically to something else.

FM This project challenges the distinction between ornament as process or product. Its system of ornamentation grows as a process of assembly and growth of a shop unit with a very particular a priori performance – the oblique display of goods. It constructs, out of an aggregate, an organization where detail or ornament is not isolated, but integral with formal and spatial effects. The opposite project in terms of detail or identity would be a hyper-differentiated skin that takes on the contingencies of each store. A strip of Amsterdam street frontage would be such an example.

SC To me this architecture has the capacity to provide for that kind of infinitely diversifiable differential pattern. The project understands that if architecture is to take command of the problem, it will do it by means of an impulse towards continuity, not the reverse. Otherwise, one would have to imitate processes that are outside architecture.

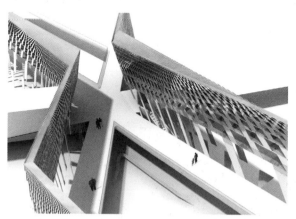

Spanish Pavilion, Aichi Expo 2005
Foreign Office Architects

Snowing in Aichi, at the close of winter

verb

❄

2°C

The same research into the potentials of ornament in built form. Like the commercial programs of the Harvard studio, the pavilions of the Aichi Expo are all "blank types": standardized blank boxes given to the architects of the different countries, who were responsible only for designing the facades and independent interior environments. Focusing on national branding on the exterior and distinct thematized atmospheres on the interior, the Spanish pavilion exploits the two primary territories of architectural conditioning: the façade (spectacle) and the bubble (atmosphere), two typologies that define many of the projects featured in this issue.

The lattice is a traditional element in Spanish architecture that reflects the fusion between Christian and Islamic cultures, while resonating with the concept of "engawa", an aspect of traditional Japanese architecture. Important sources of inspiration for our proposal are both Islamic lattices and the Gothic rose-windows and traceries found in late-gothic Spanish cathedrals in Toledo, Segovia, Seville and Palma.

One of the critical questions for the international community to address in the early 21st century is how to articulate a more productive relationship between different cultures, particularly between Western and Middle eastern cultures. This pavilion, a representation of Spain at Expo 2005 in Aichi, Japan, addresses this crucial subject through the medium of Spanish culture.

Spain occupies a unique position within this debate, as a cultural tradition that grew out of the hybridisation between the Jewish-Christian cultures of Europe and the Islamic occupation of the Iberian Peninsula between the 8th and 15th centuries. Expressing this theme in architecture, we have tried to connect the historical legacy of Spain with a vision of the future. In the design of the pavilion, we identified a repertoire of spatial organisations (courtyard types, churches and chapels), structural elements (arches and vaults) and decorative elements (lattice and traceries) that constitute the most characteristic architectural elements of this synthetic culture.

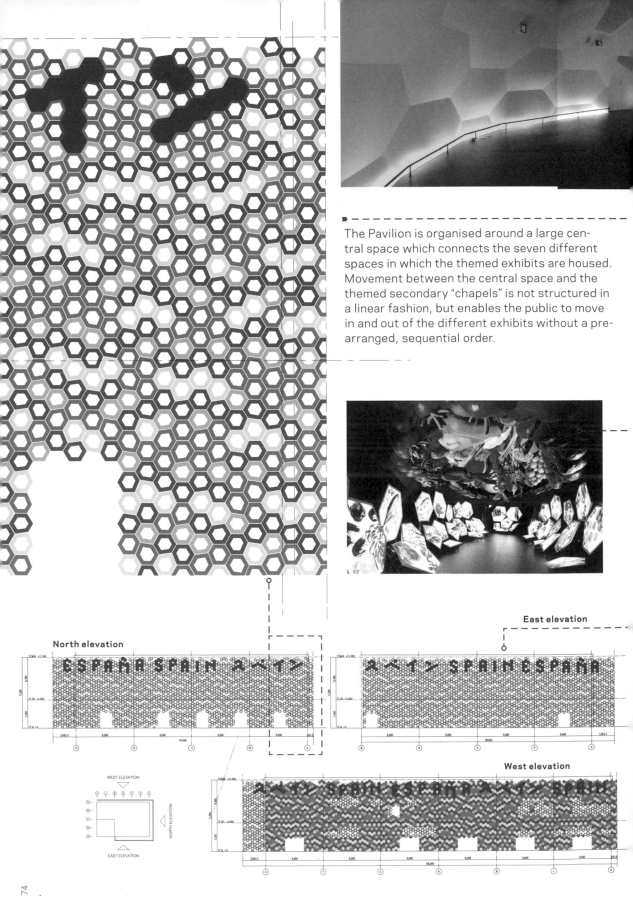

The Pavilion is organised around a large central space which connects the seven different spaces in which the themed exhibits are housed. Movement between the central space and the themed secondary "chapels" is not structured in a linear fashion, but enables the public to move in and out of the different exhibits without a prearranged, sequential order.

North elevation

ESPAÑA SPAIN スペイン

East elevation

スペイン SPAIN ESPAÑA

West elevation

スペイン SPAIN ESPAÑA スペイン SPAIN

WEST ELEVATION

NORTH ELEVATION

EAST ELEVATION

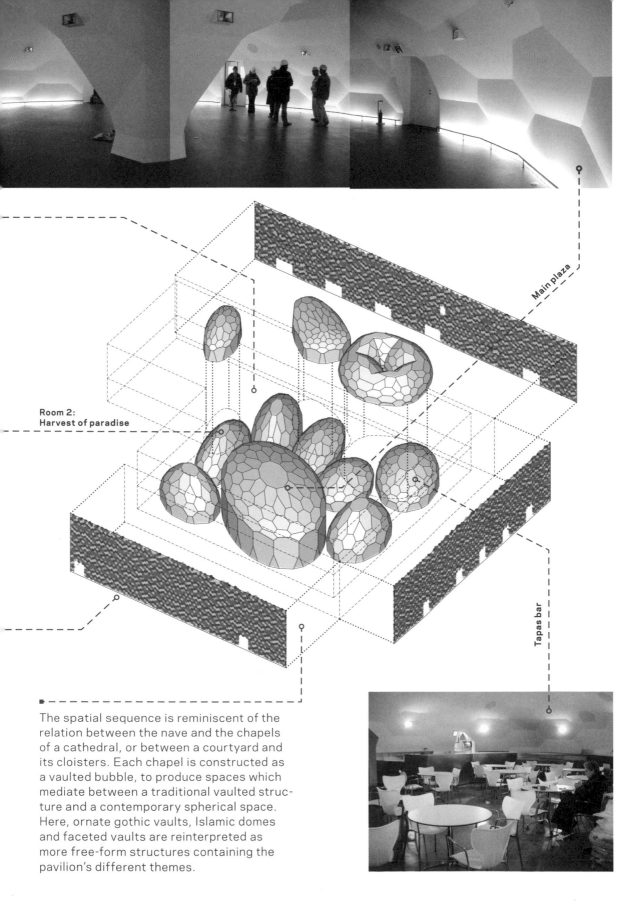

Main plaza

Room 2:
Harvest of paradise

Tapas bar

The spatial sequence is reminiscent of the relation between the nave and the chapels of a cathedral, or between a courtyard and its cloisters. Each chapel is constructed as a vaulted bubble, to produce spaces which mediate between a traditional vaulted structure and a contemporary spherical space. Here, ornate gothic vaults, Islamic domes and faceted vaults are reinterpreted as more free-form structures containing the pavilion's different themes.

We have designed a lattice consisting of six different pieces, based on a hexagonal grid (like most of gothic and Islamic tracery) and coded by color. The specificity of these pieces is such that they never repeat when assembled, producing a continuously varying pattern of geometry and color. The six colors are variations of the red and yellow of the Spanish flag, reflecting the colors internationally associated with Spain: wine, roses, blood (bullfights), sun, sand... The blocks are manufactured using glazed ceramic, a technique common in the Spanish Mediterranean coast, but also in traditional Japanese ceramics. The process of making the ceramic facade in Spain, with Spanish clay, is also literally symbolic of bringing Spanish earth to Japan.

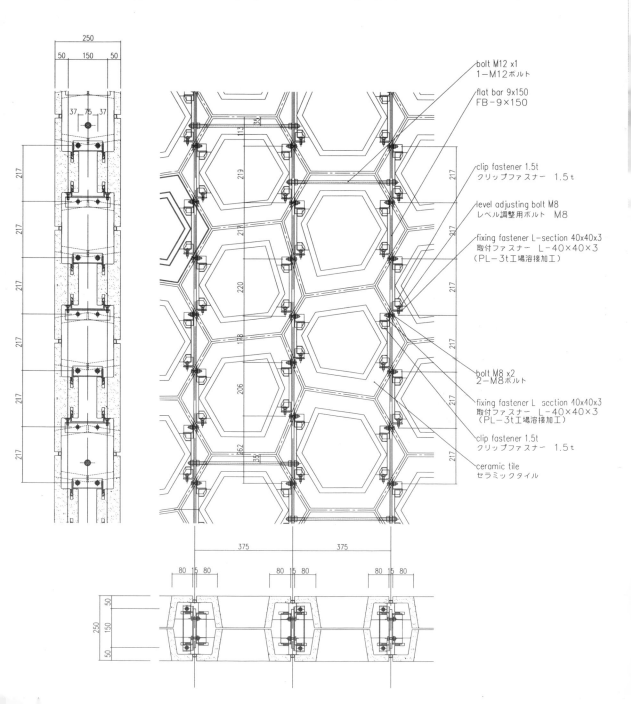

type 4

type 5

type 6

type 3

type 2

type 1

125   250   125   250   125

20   105

85   20

433

30

433   403

30

433

433

40

353   433

40

433

data

Aichi EXPO 2005. Spanish Pavillion, Aichi, Japan → Location: Ibaragabasama, Nagakute-cho, Aichi, Japan. **Client:** Sociedad Estatal para Exposiciones Internacionales (SEEI). **Design:** Farshid Moussavi and Alejandro Zaera-Polo with Nerea Calvillo, Izumi Kobayashi, Kensuke Kishikawa. **Consultants:** LOW FAT structure, M&E Consulting Engineers, Aneko Engineering Consultants Inc., Aneko Fire Research Institute. **Content designer:** INGENIA qed. **Contractor:** Takenaka Corporation Nagoya Branch. **Construction period:** September 2004 - March 2005. **Plot area:** 2,078.45 m². **Floor area:** 2,868.26 m². **Number of floors:** 2. **Structure:** Steel with concrete footing. **Building height:** 11.6m (max. building height 12.05 m). **Photographs:** Satoru Mishima. www.f-o-a.net, www.expoaichi2005.com

Flying over the outskirts of Milan, spring 2005

New Milan Trade Fair
Massimiliano Fuksas

Parking

West entrance

Pavilion

Service center

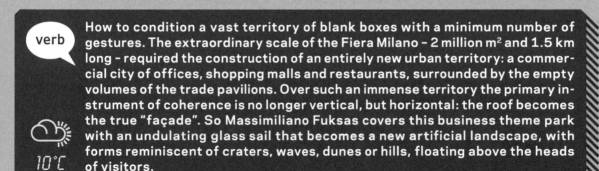

verb

10℃

How to condition a vast territory of blank boxes with a minimum number of gestures. The extraordinary scale of the Fiera Milano – 2 million m² and 1.5 km long – required the construction of an entirely new urban territory: a commercial city of offices, shopping malls and restaurants, surrounded by the empty volumes of the trade pavilions. Over such an immense territory the primary instrument of coherence is no longer vertical, but horizontal: the roof becomes the true "façade". So Massimiliano Fuksas covers this business theme park with an undulating glass sail that becomes a new artificial landscape, with forms reminiscent of craters, waves, dunes or hills, floating above the heads of visitors.

■ Service buildings

■ Sail
(Central Axis)

■ East
entrance

1500 m

The great sail of the central axis → The design of the New Milan Trade Fair makes the longitudinal axis its main generator, a connecting spine which structures the entire complex. This space, the "central axis," is the area of activities, the information center, the space of crossing, and simultaneously the place of being. These concepts are developed through a series of buildings positioned alongside the main axis, with connections at the ground level (+0.00 m) and at an upper footbridge level (+ 6.50 m). These buildings host a variety of functions: restaurants, meeting rooms, office spaces, and reception spaces which connect the exhibition halls. The pathway stretches between the east entrance and the west entrance, the main access to the Trade Fair. The buildings along the central axis hover above diverse areas of landscape – water, green areas and concrete – while the stainless steel and glass facades of the flanking exhibition halls act as scenography. The vast roof covering spans above the entire complex – an undulating lightweight, sail-like structure. The sail is over 1,300 m in length, with

a surface area exceeding 46,000 m² and an approximate width of 32 m, bordered by the facades of the pavilions lining the entire length of the central axis. The sail is comprised of a reticular rhomboidal mesh structure of pre-fabricated steel profiles, connected by spherical nodes and covered with laminated glass that is fixed to the profiles below by steel plates. The structural mesh utilises a module of 2.7 m x 2.25 m to maintain a constant width of 31.57 m along the central axis, and a width of 40.59 m along the east and the west entrances. Its height varies from +16.00 m to around +23.00 m. The mesh structure has over 32,000 nodes that create 38,929 rhomboidal frames. The entire roof is supported by 183 steel columns of 500 m diameter that split into smaller supporting arms above a height of 12 m.The form of the sail is derived from constant altimetric variations, similar to those found in naturally occurring formations such as craters, waves, dunes and hills. As a landscape the form is variegated, providing the visitor with an animated, continuously changing perspective.

From an interview with Massimiliano Fuksas by Stefano Casciani, from *Building the City of Exchange*, edited by Stefano Casciani and Anna Giorgi (Milan: Editoriale Domus/Fondazione Fiera, 2005).

I thought of a continuous stepping-up of the scale. One would "enter" into an outside scale. From this piece of city-beyond-the-city, one would access a different dimension that is difficult to perceive at first, considering the enormousness of these macrostructures. It becomes a landscape that is open to everybody; a place to go without even visiting the pavilions or the shows. You can choose whether to belong to the territory or to the urban fabric...

The weight of these glass panes is 70, 80, 120 kilos. They are the result of a very refined conception process. Then Schlaik [the engineer who heads the Mero company] arrived. Although it was late, he was still on time to design the triangularisation of the sail. Before, there were some irregular points. Now, it is perfectly triangularised. Its structure moves uniformly now, even though in some points I used the "volcanoes" to absorb the enormous forces and direct them to the ground. There are elements that are almost pure folly, such as the sail plunging down to the ground, but then shooting straight up again for 30 meters without touching it. We succeeded in building unimaginable things.

Sail → So I thought of this sail, or cloud if you prefer, that hovers above the complex. In the beginning, I was thinking that the width should be 33 meters, but its costs did not allow us to go beyond 17 meters. During the design phase I presented a model of 33 meters. Originally it was planned to be 17, but that was too narrow, and I jokingly called it the "breadstick".

Thanks to Luigi Roth, I was able to make it 33 meters. One Sunday, Roth came to my studio with Artusi. The building contractor was there too. I showed them the model that I had built of my own initiative, without being asked or paid. In front of my guests, I compared the original model, where the critical rapport between the pavilions and the sail was visible, with the second one I built of my own initiative. Roth said he preferred the new project, the one with "the small difference of costing about a hundred milliard Lire extra", and he succeeded in getting the idea accepted. During the administrational meeting, I explained the project in detail, receiving support and approval from the president.

▪ The sail is composed of 100,000 different pieces of glass.

▪ The project, which required only 27 months for the construction of 1 million m² of buildings, involved 200 designers and 2,300 workers from 62 countries.

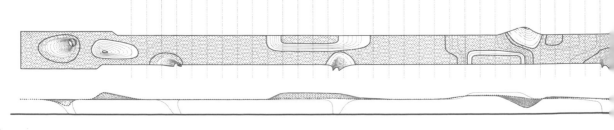

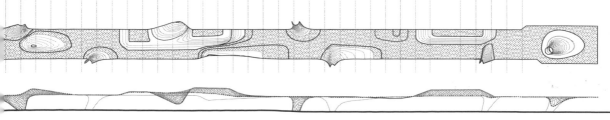

Volcanos → large skylights in the roofs of the pavilions

One might say that this is a piece of "industrial memory" that takes light from above. The "logo" is one of the most beautiful sides of the project, differentiating the scales that are present, from the very, very small to the very, very large. In order to direct this orchestra of sorts, one needs to know all the "musicians"; otherwise it proves impossible to compose the music. We know the score by heart, we know what works and what doesn't – it's like a musical problem. Maybe the sail belongs more to the world of music than to that of architecture. I could say that I took inspiration from the symphonies of Shostakovich, of whom I am a passionate fan. In his compositions, there is repetition, then a pause, then an interlude. There is absolute toughness; in the end there is exaltation.

**The total exhibition space is 530,000 m²,
a walk of 14 km from one end of the exhibition
halls to the other.**

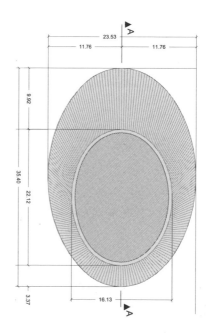

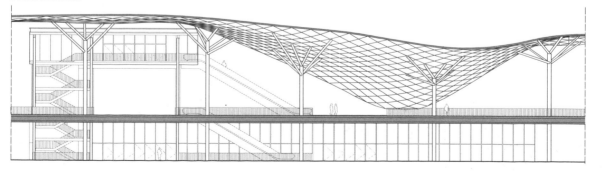

South elevation

0 5 10

Everything finishes up in the air, and "dissolving into nothing" is an important experience. It's a detail, luckily, that was experimented in Vienna. The dream is always to be able to say: "I was able to build it straight away". Clearly, it can't be this way; there must be experience.

— ▪ I extensively studied the play of reflections during the day. The reddish orange of the pavilions is reflected in the steel, making it seem like the sun is always setting.

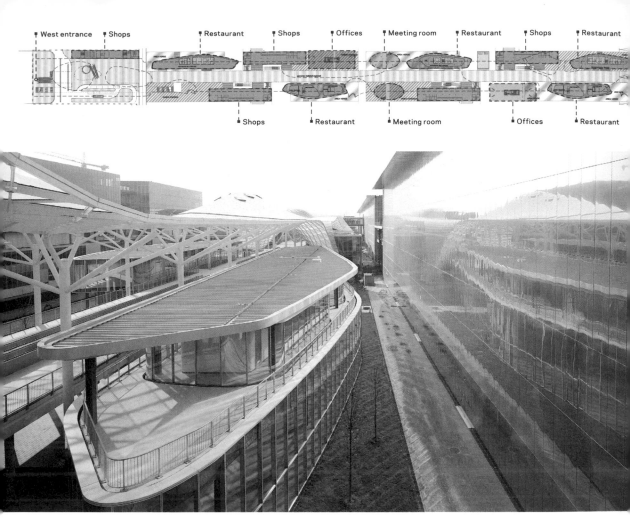

West entrance   Shops   Restaurant   Shops   Offices   Meeting room   Restaurant   Shops   Restaurant

Shops   Restaurant   Meeting room   Offices   Restaurant

Restaurant / cafe

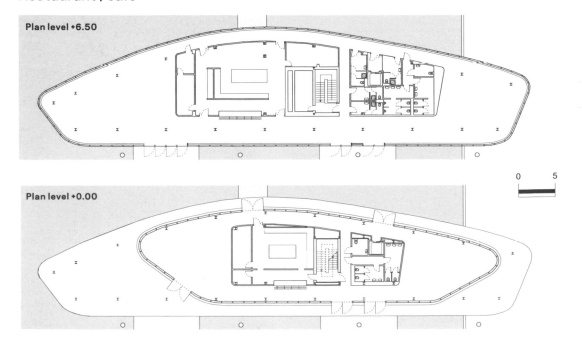

Plan level +6.50

0   5

Plan level +0.00

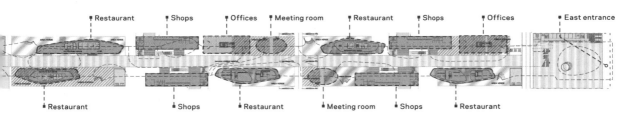

Restaurant Shops Offices Meeting room Restaurant Shops Offices East entrance

Restaurant Shops Restaurant Meeting room Shops Restaurant

Meeting room

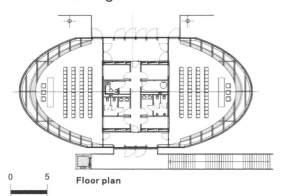

0 5

Floor plan

Section

Elevation

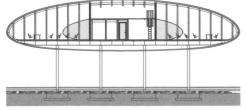

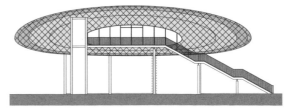

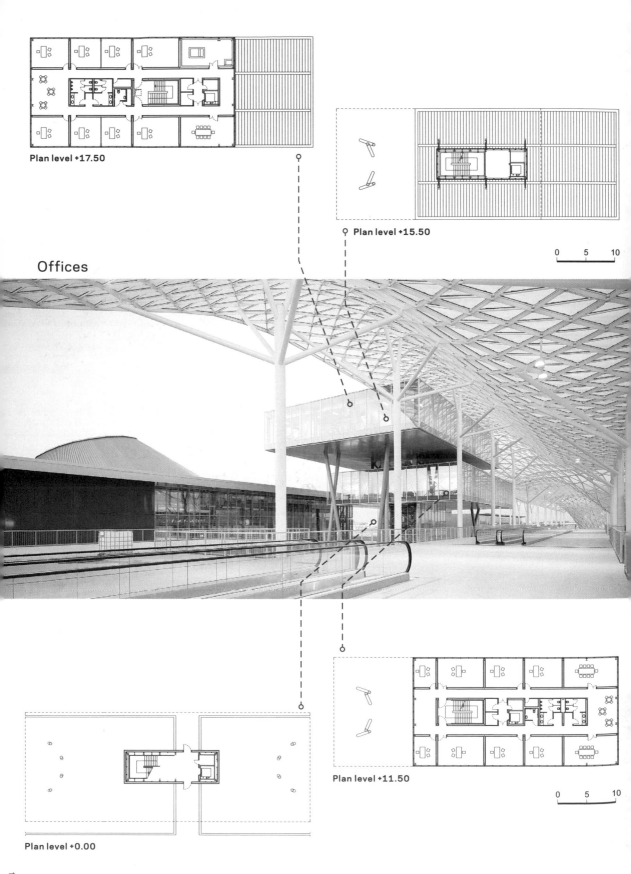

Plan level +17.50

Plan level +15.50

0   5   10

Offices

Plan level +11.50

0   5   10

Plan level +0.00

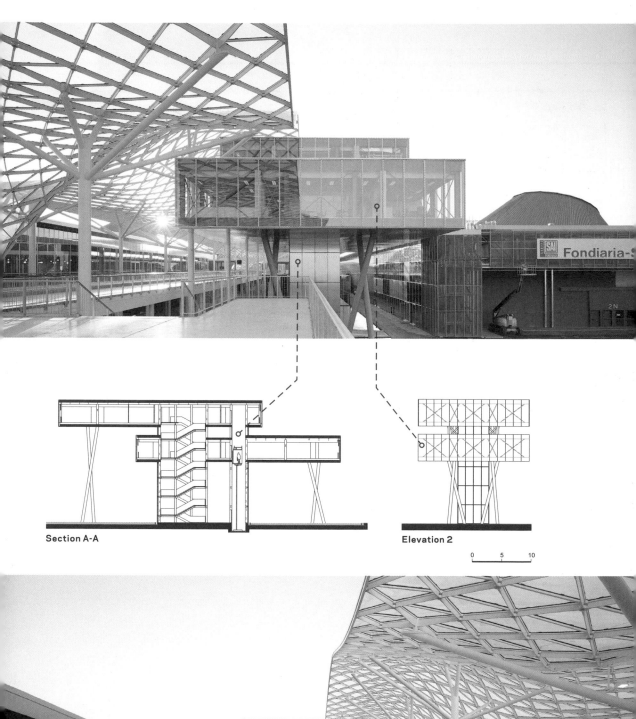

Section A-A

Elevation 2

0   5   10

Service center

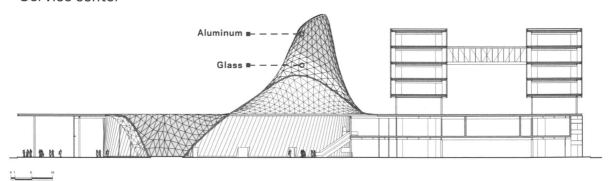

Aluminum ■ – – – –

Glass ■ – – – –

0 1   5   10

info

New Milan Trade Fair → Architect: Massimiliano Fuksas **Client:** Fondazione Fiera Milano Spa **Structure engineer:** Schlaich Bergermann und Partner (logo) **Structure engineer:** Mero GmbH & Co. (vela) **Structure consultant:** Schlaich Bergermann und Partner (vela) **Constructora/ General contractor:** Astaldi Spa, Vianini Spa, Pizzarotti Spa. **Glass roof central axis- and service center:** MERO GmbH & Co. **Curtain walls:** Permasteelisa spa **Steel structure:** Icom Engineering, Ask Romein, Carpentieri d'Italia **Roof:** Bemo Systems **Lighting:** Lampada Lavinia, de / by Doriana y / and Massimiliano Fuksas para / for iGuzzini **Pavilion Executive design:** Studio Altieri **Civil engineer:** Arch. Francesco Marzullo **Designer and art director:** Doriana O. Mandrelli **Project architects:** Giorgio Martocchia, Angelo Agostini, Ralf Bock. **3D:** Fabio Cibinel. **Project team:** Angelo Agostani, Fabrizio Arrigoni, Chiara Baccarini, giulio Baiocco, Daniele Biondi, Giuseppe Blengini, Laura Buonfrate, Sofia Cattinari, Irene Ciampi, Chiara Costanzelli, Alberto Greti, Kentaro Kimizuca, Roberto Laurenti, Davide Marchetti, Luca Maugeri, Dominique Raptis, Cesare Rivera, Adele Savino, Tasja Tesche, Toyohiko Yamaguchi. **Construction period:** 27 meses / months **End of construction:** 2 abril /April 2005 **Total surface area:** 2.000.000 m² **Built area:** 1.000.000 m² **Length of central axis:** 1.500 m **Parking capacity:** 20.050 coches / cars **Truck parking capacity:** 7.000 **Exhibition parking area:** 4.320 coches / cars

"Biosphere 2 is a manmade closed ecological system in Oracle, Arizona built by Edward P. Bass, Space Biosphere Ventures and others. Constructed between 1987 and 1989, It was used to test if and how people could live and study in a closed biosphere, while carrying out scientific experiments. It explored the possible use of closed biospheres in space colonization, and also allowed the study and manipulation of a biosphere without harming Earth's. The name comes from the idea that it is modelled on 'Biosphere 1' - Earth." ◀ – → **http://en.wikipedia.org/wiki/Biosphere_2**

East Lung

West Lung

Biosphere 2
Edward P. Bass, Space Biosphere Ventures

verb

45℃

To artificially recreate nature is not a new desire. The baroque park is already the refined scenification of the landscape. In the 20th century there emerges the material possibility of fabricating a completely independent, artificial biosphere destined for long interplanetary trips. Four terrestrial landscapes enclosed in a dome in the middle of the Arizona desert. (For example, a copy of the desert in the middle of the desert.) What turned out to be a mistake and a fiasco that would later be recuperated for science, and for consumption. Like the Eden Project, Biosphere 2 serves at once as laboratory and theme park.

Somewhere in the Arizona desert, USA

Agricultural Area

Desert

Marsh

Savannah

Ocean

Rain Forest

Eden Project | Cornwall, UK | 1

15 years after Biosphere 2, a second man-made nature was constructed in Cornwall, UK. Rather than housing experimental facilities like Biosphere 2, Eden was conceived as an an environmental theme park, with botanical gardens, a museum and an education center. Following its opening in 2001, 1.8 million people visit every year, making it one of the most popular tourist spots in England. The world's largest geodesic dome contains plants from around the world in their natural micro-climates, like those of Malaysia, South Africa, the Mediterranean and California.

Photo: Nick Gregory / APEX

1 Humid Tropics Biome (Tropical Islands, Malaysia, West Africa, Tropical South America) **2** Outdoor Biome (Cornwall and British temperate regions, parts of America, Russia and Indian foothills) **3** Warm Temperate Biome (the Mediterranean Basin, South Africa, California)

Eden Project | Cornwall, UK 2

The biggest greenhouse in the world
To enclose the largest amount of space economically, the Eden project is composed of
a chain of geodesic domes.
Photo: Simon Burt / APEX

Why this shape?
Efficient: maximum size and strength
with minimum steel.
Energy saving: maximum volume with
minimum surface area (minimizes
heat loss).
Adaptable: moulds to the shape of the site.
Lightweight: the weight of the steel is
almost the same as the weight of air it
encloses.
Roomy: spans 110 meters at its widest
point with no internal supports – allowing
complete freedom for the plants and
the interior landscapes.

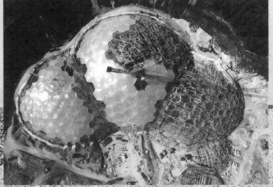

Built with $150 million in funding from Texas oil magnate Edward Bass, Biosphere 2 was designed as an air-tight replica of Earth's environment (Biosphere 1). This 7,200,000-cubic-foot [203,880 m³] sealed glass and space-frame structure contains 5 biomes, including a 900,000-gallon [4,091,480 liter] ocean, a rain forest, a desert, agricultural areas and a human habitat. Some of the early designers and managers were interested in space travel and the possibility of colonizing the Moon or Mars. By building Biosphere 2 and sealing people inside, they hoped to learn what problems would arise from living in a closed system. So it was that in 1991, a colony of 8 people set about to live inside Biosphere 2 for two years. The first crew of Biospherians (4 women and 4 men) entered Biosphere 2 on September 26, 1991. The crew members remained inside for two years and stopped on September 26, 1993.

▪— → http://www.desertusa.com/mag99/apr/stories/bios2.html

Eden Project | Cornwall, UK | 3

Light, strong and resistive ETFE covers the domes instead of glass

The domes are built of galvanised tubular steel hexagons that are approximately 9m across. Because glass would be too heavy, too inflexible and too dangerous, the frames are covered with a triple layer of ETFE (Ethylene Tetra Fluoro Ethylene Co-Polymer) foil. ETFE is:

> highly transparent
(lets UV light through)
> a better insulator than glass
> not degraded by sunlight
> strong and light
(weighs less than 1% of glass,
and so requires less steel structure)
> recyclable
> lasts at least 30 years
> anti-static, and non-stick, therefore self cleaning (guaranteed maintenance-free for 25 years).

In all, 831 panels cover the biomes: 625 hexagons (410 in the HT biome and 215 in the WT biome), 16 pentagons (5 in HTB, 11 in WTB), 190 triangular vents (90 in HTB, 100 in WTB), with 7,294,685 kg of steel.

How big are the Biomes?

Humid Tropics Biome → 15,590 sm (1.55 hectares), 55 meters high, 100 meters wide, 200 meters long

Warm Temperate Biome → 6,540 sm (0.65 hectares), 35 meters high, 65 meters wide, 135 meters long

> Erecting the covered biomes required the world's largest bird-cage scaffolding system: 12 levels, 25 meters across, and 46,000 poles, totaling 370 km of scaffolding.
> The largest biome is big enough to house the Tower of London.
> The largest hexagon is 10.98 meters across from point to point, large enough to contain a London taxi.
> There are 5,861,995 kg of air: a volume of 330,110m³ inside the HT biome and a volume of 85,620m³ inside the WT biome.

On ETFE foils Photo: Simon Burt / APEX

Why did Biospere 2 fail only after two years?

Lack of oxygen → In spite of calculations that the air rate would be stable, factors like bacteria in the soil caused the rate of oxygen to drop over time. Lack of sunlight also reduced levels of photosynthesis, increasing the chronic lack of oxygen.

Lack of CO_2 → As oxygen level decrease, CO_2 has to increase to aid photosynthesis. It was discovered that CO_2 was absorbed by the concrete walls of the building.

Lack of food → Many plants did not grow well due to the lack of oxygen and sunlight. Most of the animals died as their diet became poorer and poorer. Undernourished team members were supposedly overjoyed by a mere harvest of coffee.

Psychological distress → When people are put in sealed spaces completely disconnected from the outside, emotions can become unstable and can cause conflict. The chronic lack of food and doubts about safety only increased this distress.

Eden Project Cornwall, UK 4

Photo: Simon Burt / APEX

Plants → Over 100,000 plants representing 5,000 species from many of the climatic zones of the world. Many of these can grow in the mild conditions of Cornwall, others demand greenhouses and that is where Eden's two gigantic conservatories come in. The Humid Tropics Biome – the world's largest greenhouse – is home to the plants of the rainforest – bananas, rubber, cocoa, coffee, teak and mahogany. Whilst the warm Temperate Biome is filled with the plants of the Mediterranean regions of the world – South Africa, California and the Med itself. Outside sunflowers, hemp, tea and a host of other plants from our own region grow.

Animals → Only certain birds (that fit in with the Biome environment), certain insects and reptiles, e.g. geckos. Many of these will be used as biological controls to control the pests.

Waste Neutral → As part of our sustainability strategy we're tackling resource and waste management. After reducing and reusing Eden aims to buy in a greater weight of products made from recycled materials than the weight of materials we send off to be recycled and thus become 'Waste Neutral.'

Water → At the bottom of the pit Eden is 15 m below the water table, so without a state-of-the-art drainage and pumping system. The 'grey' water is collected and used for irrigation and flushing toilets. The rain falling on the Biomes is collected, treated and then used for irrigation and humidification within the greenhouses.

Humidity → In the Humid Tropics we keep it up with automated misting nozzles (90% at night, and down to 60% during visiting hours). In the Warm Temperate we keep it down; vents are often open, even during relatively cool periods, to reduce humidity close to the leaves.

Temperature → The main heating source for both Biomes is the sun. The back wall acts as a heat bank, releasing warmth at night. The two layers of air in the triple-glazed windows give maximum insulation. Extra heating is provided through the air-handling units, the big grey boxes outside the Biomes. The Humid Tropics Biome ranges from 18°C to 35°C; and the Warm Temperate, 25°C to a winter minimum of about 10°C.

Ventilation → The vents may seem small for a building this large. They work because the height generates a 'chimney effect' that draws air through the system. On very hot days the air-handling units help circulate the air within the Biomes.

Position → Keen gardeners know that south facing lean-to greenhouses are the business as far as keeping the heat in is concerned. The back wall acts as a heat bank, taking in the sun in the day and releasing the heat at night. Here they went a step further, a 3D profile of the pit was fed into a computer in a 'solar animation study'. The computer pinpointed the exact 'hot spot' in which to put the Biomes. The amount of air in the pillows can be adjusted. On a hot day they can be deflated as air expands and if cold, air can be pumped in – a living building.

After a 6 month transition period, a second trial began with a team of 7 "biospherians" (5 men and 2 women). Again a number of physical and social problems soon developed, and the project suffered scientific disdain and public ridicule before the experiments were suspended in 1994. Since then, there have been no resident crews living inside Biosphere 2, and no future human habitation is planned. In 1995, management of Biosphere 2 was transferred to Columbia University. The next year, the building opened to visitors as a science center. Since then over 1200 graduate students have spent a year in the Biosphere 2 Center, and more than 2 million tourists have visited. As of January 2005, the campus is for sale. Decisions Investments Corporation, the owners of Biosphere 2, have announced they are looking for prospective buyers like universities, churches, resorts, or spas.

verb

Through advances like an artificial wind system and UV pass-through filters for the growth of plants, the Eden Project has solved some of the problems that doomed Biosphere 2 to failure. So these two attempts to artificially recreate the environmental processes of nature – one designed for serious scientific experiments and resurrected as an eco-theme park, the second built as a commercial enterprise – have very different histories. Because of its unusual size and lightness, the Eden Project is now being considered as a possible model for a space colony on Mars: the original purpose of Biosphere 2, realized 15 years later.

The Stimulus Progression:
Muzak and the Culture of Horizontality

AUDC / Robert Sumrell and Kazys Varnelis

 23°C

verb

In the 21st century, architecture – a discipline for the production of atmo-spheres and experiences – has been challenged by the invention of technolo-gies that allow the production of increasingly extensive effects with ever more minimal means. Like the trajectory of Archigram or Superstudio in the 1970's, where spectacular large-scale architectures give way to individual-ized environments (like Reyner Banham's environment bubble) or to minimal, equipped surfaces on which any kind of activity can take place, today an in-creasingly sophisticated micro-technology of effects (like Bluetooth or the iPod, but also micro-films that can regulate temperature and luminosity in architectural environments) is reducing the traditional importance of built form as a tool for controlling spatial experience. Here we begin a survey of this new world of micro-effects with AUDC's history of Muzak, the first vir-tual technology for moduating physical behaviors and environments.

Music is the perfect commodity. While the spectacle is capital accumulated to the degree that it becomes image, music takes this process a step further.

Visibility is, for us, a thing of the past. Just as for Hegel philosophy took over the role of art, today code matters more than form. Over 30 years ago, Andrea Branzi pointed out that under Late Capitalism, Capital and the City have colonized the world, and, therefore, lacking any exterior, neither needs to strive relentlessly to become visible anymore. Instead, the smooth and continuous operation of the system itself becomes the problem. This is clearly demonstrated by the lessening importance of the skyline in the most highly developed countries and the rising dominance of the Internet in its stead. Ours is a world of machine languages, transmission protocols, console dumps, signal-processing codecs, ISBN, UPC. The world that surrounds us is made up of code.

Music is the prototype for all code. Capable of forks, bifurcations, and looping behaviors, codes and music are temporal processes, invisible and inert until decoded or performed. In their modern commodity forms, music and code are endlessly reproducible.

Music first becomes a commodity with Thomas Edison's development of the phonograph in 1877, which played back sound from a rotating cylinder, and the related development, a decade later, of Emile Berliner's gramophone, which replaced the cylinder with a revolving disc. Through these devices, consumers could control their audio programming and listen to their favorite songs repeatedly. The packaging of Edison's cylinders led consumers to call the new medium "canned music." The weary worker could relax at home and listen to songs on demand, without expending effort.

The experience of listening to recorded music is a distinct experience from producing music or going to a concert. The ease of playback allows the listener to perceive the music through distraction, not through active contemplation. Moreover, while listening to music in one's own home undid the old experience of communal musical appreciation, the mass distribution of a single, recorded piece allowed dispersed communities to form around the appreciation of music.

The appearance of mass-produced music at the turn of the century came at a moment when leisure time was expanding and posing new problems for the recently invented profession of the manager. While the factory and office demanded new levels of attention from the worker, they also created new heights of monotony. Both the workday and the workweek shortened so that employees could have time to recover from their dull labors. But leisure time had its own dangers: the working class could fall prey either to destabilizing mass-oriented political forces or to drink and unruly individual behavior. Welfare organizations such as the YMCA sprang up to help workers, while corporations created organized recreational activities such as sports and adult education. To teach workers lasting values and to make the workplace more humane, corporations established programs in which workers either listened to or produced music. At Frank Lloyd Wright's Larkin Administration Building in Buffalo, a pipe organ and reproducing piano were installed so that musicians could play for the young secretaries who worked there. Henry Ford hired the Detroit

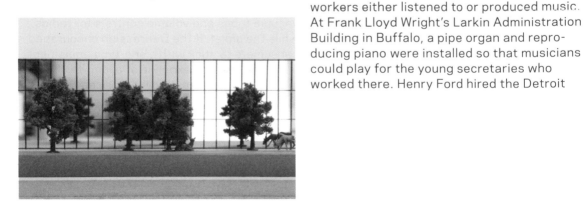

Symphony to play for his employees several times a year. Other corporations incorporated organized music directly into the workplace. Department stores held morning sing-alongs in order to instill politeness in their workers. All this took time out from leisure and allowed a conditioning of the workers' lives.

The Wired Wireless Mass Medium →

The invention of radio at the beginning of the twentieth century further transformed the individual's relationship to the collective by providing a system for instantaneous verbal communication across great distances. During the 1920's, commercial radio broadcasts spread across radio waves provided regular, dependable media experiences that large numbers of individuals could share simultaneously, even while apart. Once purchased, radios assembled these individuals into a mass audience regardless of their literacy or social status, creating the first true mass media. Through the addition of the tuning dial, radio listeners gained the effortless experience of surfing for information from different channels and the ability to choose between programs for the first time. Listening to the radio was less a private experience enjoyed by an autonomous individual, and more a series of individual or small group experiences in which people saw themselves as part of a regionally dispersed body made up of content producers, transmitters, radio signals, receivers, and other listeners whom they would likely never meet.

Radio, however, still faced many real limitations: it required large and expensive signal towers while its relatively weak transmissions would degrade in poor weather conditions, were easily interrupted by local terrain, and dropped off due to distance.

In 1911, General George Squier discovered a solution to these problems, finding an effective means of audio transmission over electrical power lines using the signal multiplexing he developed to carry multiple channels over one wire. In contrast to wireless radio, transmitting music through the system Squier named "wired wireless" ensured higher signal quality regardless of atmospheric or solar conditions. Weary of the privatization that had marred the early development of the telephone industry, Squier patented his discovery in the name of the American public, making the technology available for free use and development across the nation.

Engineers adapted the new technology to create the first countrywide communications network allowing the simultaneous delivery of programs through utility lines to remote radio transmitting stations. Squier, however, was not satisfied with the commercial structure of radio, in which programs were funded by intrusive commercials. He hoped to create a new network supported by a toll that would also make unnecessary the commercials and program interruptions that sponsored, and in Squier's mind corrupted, radio. Squier approached the North American Company, then the nation's largest utility company, to transmit music over their lines. North American responded positively and formed Wired Radio, Incorporated. To avoid problems with broadcast rights to music, North American purchased Breitkopf Publications, Inc., a European music-publishing house, and renamed it Associated Music Publishers.

But wired wireless was not initially successful. Radios quickly became more appealing with the development of superheterodyne circuits, vacuum tubes and volume controls for radios, while the onset of the Depression encouraged consumers to stick with a one-time equipment purchase over the expense of a long-term lease. Nevertheless, North American persevered and, in 1934, formed the Muzak Corporation to transmit music directly to homes in Cleveland. Muzak's name was derived from a merger of the word "music" with "Kodak," which was, by that time, widely regarded as a highly technological and reputable company. Squier died later that year, never to see the success of his invention.

Success was not, in any case, immediate. The project in Cleveland fell victim to technological troubles. Moreover, radio companies opposed the idea of Muzak being broadcast into homes. In 1938, the Federal Communications Commission severely restricted Muzak's market by forbidding it from using electrical power lines for broadcast directly into the home. Although Squier's inventions of wired wireless and signal multiplexing would later be widely adopted by cable television broadcasters, Muzak would initially be restricted to commercial venues.

Targeting commercial venues offered the Muzak Corporation an unseen advantage. Recorded music is sold with limited rights of use. Recorded media was an enormous source of income for the young record industry, but created new difficulties in tracking the number and locations of its playback. In 1914, the American Society of Composers, Artists, and Publishers (ASCAP) was founded, serving as a member-owned organization that fought for the fair compensation of the music industry for the public performance of recorded work. The first successful lawsuit pursued by ASCAP, against Shanley's Restaurant in New York City, was heard by the United States Supreme Court. Closing the trial, Justice Oliver Wendell Holmes explained his judgment in favor of ASCAP by saying "If music did not pay, it would be given up. Whether it pays or not, the purpose of employing it is profit and that is enough."

By 1920, the administration of music rights had become a major business. While radio stations could license programming for personal performance, they could not track where music was being played and take responsibility for its licensing. The wired wireless subscription service, however, was ideal for this task. Because every Muzak receiver had to have a corresponding receiver set, it was easy for Muzak to track who was using their service and exactly what the service was being used for.

Muzak re-formed in New York City and began to cater to the hotel and restaurant market in such famed venues as the Chambord, the Stork Club, and the Waldorf Astoria. Audio would subsequently be sent to clubs through leased telephone lines rather than electric lines. Speakers would be hidden amongst large plants, thereby making the music seem to come out of nowhere and lending it the name "potted palm" music. With the disappearance of any visible means of sound production, Muzak exceeded the gramophone's capacity to make sound autonomous.

Muzak also delivered programming to the workplace, where it soothed the minds of employees, enhancing their productivity while eliminating the distractions caused by commercials, scripted programs, and other verbal content, as well as to New York City apartment buildings, where it was allowed as a service that enhanced the quality of life.

Elevator Music → Sending music to the workplace was in keeping with the vision that Squier had left for the company. As Chief Signal Officer of the US Army Signal Corps, Squier used music to increase the productivity of his secretaries, Afterwards, he investigated ways to use music to recapture the benefits of pre-industrial song, in order to soothe the nerves of employees while increasing their output. The idea of using music to improve an environment was not uncommon by the 1930's, when dentists used music to augment or even replace anesthetic.

Starting also in the 1930's, the Hawthorne Effect, named after a study at the Hawthorne Plant of the Western Electric Company in Cicero, Illinois, provided a rationale for human relations in the workplace. The Hawthorne Effect simply concluded that individuals would be more productive when they knew they were being studied or paid attention to, regardless of the experimental manipulation employed. The Hawthorne studies suggested that the workplace was, first and foremost, a social system made up of interdependent parts. According to this theory workers are more influenced by social demands from inside and outside the workplace, by their need for recognition, security, and a sense of belonging, than by the physical environment that surrounds them. Being the object of a study made workers feel involved and important.

Early Muzak featured an unreflective programming that mimicked radio, with a hotel orchestra sound developed by Ben Selvin, a prolific bandleader who had recorded 1,000 records by 1924 and whose Moulin Rouge Orchestra had extensive experience in early radio. Named vice-president for recording and programming at the corporation in 1934, Selvin developed programming ideal for Muzak at this stage.

The music provider acted much as a radio station, with distinct programs featuring types of music such as marches for breakfast and pipe organs for lunch. Selvin preferred a quiet and restrained sound with few brass instruments and an emphasis on strings. Muzak provided a gesture to the workers – deploying the Hawthorne Effect – a constant reminder that the boss was thinking of them. To prevent the music from lulling workers to sleep, however, Selvin chose popular songs familiar to everyone, thereby keeping workers' attention. Within the workplace, Muzak distinguished between four basic conditions – public areas, offices, light industrial settings, and heavy industrial settings – each of which would be addressed by a different music program. In industrial settings, where loud noises make traditional background music hard to hear, Muzak turned to sounds with a greater penetration, favoring percussion instruments and melodies with more distinct timbres. Even if the factory was loud, the difference in pitch made the music audible. Studies produced by Muzak showed that it reduced absenteeism in the workplace by 88 percent.

Muzak soon proved useful in locations beyond the office or factory floor. As skyscrapers grew ever taller in North American cities, building owners employed Muzak to calm anxious elevator riders; quickly earning Muzak's programs the name "elevator music."

The Stimulus Progression → During the twentieth century wars were key catalysts for technological and social advancement. In the First World War, Squier significantly advanced the radio and the airplane, while the principles of Taylorism and Fordism spread widely in industry both in the United States and abroad. During the Second World War, the military sponsored scientific research and stimulated management techniques to improve productivity, including extensive research into the playing of music in office and factory environments. These studies, often conducted by employees of Muzak and its competitors, concluded that silence during repetitive tasks led to boredom, while talking was too distracting. Music, on the other hand, did not draw the eye's attention away from the task at hand but alleviated fatigue arising from monotonous actions.

The general conclusion of these studies suggested that music affects the body physiologically, stimulating breathing, metabolism, muscular energy, pulse, blood pressure, and internal secretions. This fit neatly with the James-Lange theory which suggested ways to influence emotions, a popular subject during wartime. Developed independently by William James and Carl Lange, the James-Lange theory states that the human nervous system creates automatic changes with regard to experiences in the world. Only once one feels a rise in heart rate, an increase in perspiration, dryness of the mouth, and so on does one experience emotion. By affecting the body physiologically, background music could keep workers' nervous systems calm and thereby give them greater emotional stability during the difficult days of wartime.

Starting during the "baptism by fire" of the British during 1940, the BBC's "Music While You Work" program broadcast music made by two live bands to factories daily to prevent workers from dwelling on their predicament and to soothe them upon returning to work after a night of bombing. Soon after, music was made mandatory for all British war workers. By 1943, some 6 million American workers listened to music in the factory provided by Muzak, RCA, General Electric or other audio programming providers, and by war's end some 5 million British workers listened to "Music While You Work."

After the war, corporations continued to be interested in using music to improve productivity. At Muzak, company researchers who had been involved in wartime research came to the conclusion that, in addition to the vague increase in productivity that music in the workplace created according to the Hawthorne Effect, the James-Lange theory suggested that music could more deliberately affect the changing attention levels of workers throughout the day to maintain a steady level of productivity. While Taylorist work practices streamlined industrial manufactur-

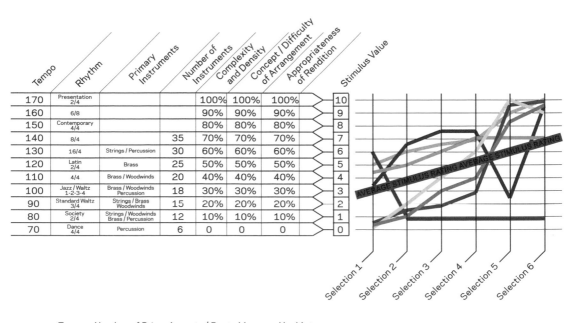

Tempo	Rhythm	Primary Instruments	Number of Instruments	Complexity and Density	Concept / Difficulty of Arrangement	Appropriateness of Rendition	Stimulus Value
170	Presentation 2/4			100%	100%	100%	10
160	6/8			90%	90%	90%	9
150	Contemporary 4/4			80%	80%	80%	8
140	8/4		35	70%	70%	70%	7
130	16/4	Strings / Percussion	30	60%	60%	60%	6
120	Latin 2/4	Brass	25	50%	50%	50%	5
110	4/4	Brass / Woodwinds	20	40%	40%	40%	4
100	Jazz / Waltz 1-2-3-4	Brass / Woodwinds Percussion	18	30%	30%	30%	3
90	Standard Waltz 3/4	Strings / Brass Woodwinds	15	20%	20%	20%	2
80	Society 2/4	Strings / Woodwinds Brass / Percussion	12	10%	10%	10%	1
70	Dance 4/4	Percussion	6	0	0	0	0

AVERAGE STIMULUS RATING AVERAGE STIMULUS RATING

Selection 1 — Selection 2 — Selection 3 — Selection 4 — Selection 5 — Selection 6

Tempo - Number of Prime Accents / Beats Measured by Metronome
Rhythm - Musical Form / Broad Classifications of Popular Music
Predominant Instrumental Useage
Number of Instruments Used in Arrangement
Complexity and Density / Stimulus Through Arrangement Methods
Conceptual Rigor / Nature of Melody and Harmony Combined to Make a Musical Point
Appropriateness of Rendition in Reference to the Original Arrangement

ing and office work, they also made these jobs even more monotonous. Without direct supervision, the fatigue and boredom brought about by repetitive tasks could quickly undo the very advances that these new practices hoped to provide. Muzak researchers concluded that varying the tempo of music played to workers throughout the workday was one way of fighting fatigue. According to one of the fundamental observations of modern industrial psychology, the Yerkes-Dodson Law, first developed by Robert M. Yerkes and John D. Dodson in 1908, optimal performance is attained with a median level of arousal. Too much arousal distracts the worker while too little leads to inertia. The sources of arousal in the office environment can take many forms, and include negative stimuli like stress and anxiety as well as pleasure and comfort or even, as the Hawthorne Effect proved, the act of scientific monitoring itself. The key is not each moment of arousal itself, but the flow from one moment to the next, and the variation of arousal types. Complex work is inherently more engaging and therefore requires less distraction from background music, while simple work, being less arousing, requires a greater degree of complexity from the music. Whatever the workplace environment, Muzak set out to maintain a median level of arousal. Muzak observed that natural levels of arousal are never static or consistently varied, but rise and fall throughout the day as well as over fifteen minute cyclical periods. In response, Muzak arranged programs according to a "Stimulus Progression," varying musical energy levels over fifteen-minute segments that would be followed by either a thirty-second or fifteen-minute long period of silence, depending on the subscriber's desire. The Stimulus Progression was based on Muzak's analysis of its songs for their emotional content and energy levels. Factoring in tempo, type of music, instruments employed, and the size of the orchestra, Muzak determined a stimulus value for each song. By the 1950s, Muzak could carefully vary its level of stimulus during the day to offset decreases in worker efficiency during mid-morning and mid-afternoon slumps. The fifteen-minute length of the Stimulus Progression also served to enhance productivity by creating more distinctly delimited breaks between spurts of work activity. The order of the Stimulus Progression was crucial: studies showed that if played backwards, it would put listeners to sleep.

The Stimulus Progression was based on the human heartbeat. Playing music at a rate above that of the heartbeat – an average of 72 beats per minute at rest – stimulated the individual, but constantly doing so would make them nervous. Thus, the Stimulus Progression would start out below 72 bpm and rise above that rate. That the Stimulus Progression addressed the heartbeat at rest underscores that Muzak focused not so much on the factory, where workers might exert themselves, but on the office, which had its heyday in the postwar era and where workers would be sedentary.

Programmed for round-the-clock shifts, Muzak created an endless circadian cycle in which all sounds, including silence, were given space. Eventually, Muzak began to develop additional programs for use in homes, hospitals, urban environments, government facilities, and outdoor spaces. With its omnipresence, Muzak could order our lives temporally.

In "Postscript on the Societies of Control," Gilles Deleuze traces the transition from a society of discipline to a society of control. As both Bataille and Foucault point out, architecture was the instrument for discipline and order throughout the Eighteenth and nineteenth centuries. As a device for creating enclosure and allowing for the supervision of many workers by a few managers, buildings structured society. By the middle of the twentieth century, however, this model no longer held power. In place of the 'molds' made by enclosures, Deleuze states that we are entering into a time of modulations. Instead of fear, work is now based on identifying with and entering the flow. The Stimulus Progression ensured the success of modulation in the workplace.

"Muzak Fills the Deadly Silences" → Muzak developed during the era of "jazzy" design and Art Deco architecture. Like Art Deco, Muzak was meant to inspire office workers to move along to the increasingly fast pace of the modern corporation. Just as design and architecture evolved from Art Deco to the International Style, Muzak moved to the Stimulus Progression.

The streamlined geometry of Art Deco design attempted to mask the repetitive nature of office work with a representation of the speed and tempo of modern music. But Art Deco failed to keep its promise: being fixed into architectural form, it could only represent change, and was not itself capable of changing over time. As workers grew accustomed to Art Deco, they grew bored of it and began to associate it with bygone eras, not with the present.

As International Style architecture spread in the postwar era, Muzak spread with it. Muzak punctuated activity on the floors of the Johnson Wax Company building, Lever House, the Seagram building, the Chase Manhattan bank building, the Pan Am building, the Sears Tower, the Apollo XI command module and countless other modernist buildings. Muzak is the hidden element in every Ezra Stoller photograph of a modernist office interior. By 1950, some 50 million people heard Muzak every year.

Modernism needed Muzak. The new, hermetically sealed office buildings permitted by the glass curtain wall and the postwar air conditioning system were capable of blocking out distracting sounds from outside, but silence itself could be noticeable. Muzak ensured a background condition even greater than that of silence itself.

Muzak's slogan during this period was "Muzak fills the deadly silences." But Muzak isn't just invisible to the eyes; in the company's own words, Muzak "is meant to be heard, but not listened to," and is aimed at a subliminal level. The immaterial gestures of the Stimulus Progression were neither ornamental nor representational, but rather physiological. Workers do not think about Muzak; they are

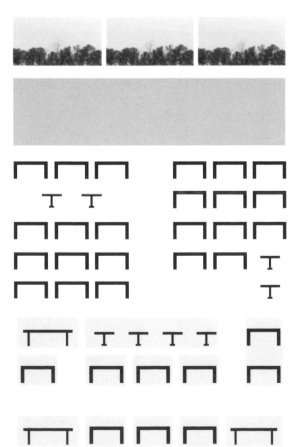

programmed by it. Whenever Muzak received any requests for songs, they immediately removed them from the library. Like the Fordist worker, Muzak that drew attention to itself was deemed unsuccessful and dismissed.

By filling the deadly silences, Muzak supported modernism and made the impersonality of the Fordist management system more palatable. In bridging melody (individuality) and monotony (the abstract field), Muzak provides an element of accommodation against a background of abstraction, acting as a palliative for both the modern office and modern architecture. Interactions between individuals that would otherwise have been uncomfortable, such as disciplinary reprimands, terminations and general office tension, could all be alleviated by its soothing background tones.

Thus, when James Keenen, Ph.D., the Chairman of Muzak's Board of Scientific Advisors, stated that "Muzak promotes the sharing of meaning because it massifies symbolism in which not few but all can participate," we need to understand that Muzak provided the same symbolic experience as the pre-Industrial song did; however, this sharing of meaning happened not consciously, but just below the threshold of consciousness. Composed almost exclusively of love songs stripped of their lyrics, the Stimulus Progression provided a gentle state of erotic arousal throughout the day. Desire, union and disappointment could all be felt collectively, even though subconsciously, thereby adding color to the day and blunting the impact of these emotions when real life intruded into the workplace.

Whereas in the 1930's Muzak was essentially the same as popular music and radio, by the 1940's it had gone its own way, creating a different level of attention and its own medium. Muzak had pioneered the use of long playing 33 1/3 rpm records in order to create more seamless soundscapes for its functional music. In contrast, RCA Victor's 1949 introduction of the smaller and less expensive 45 rpm disc format allowed popular hits and youth-oriented rock music to be taken almost anywhere and listened to over and over.

One of the most important consumer objects of the twentieth century, record players helped to create radically new communities based on consumption and consumer identity, rather than work itself. After a tremendous period of economic and technological growth from the first two world wars, a surplus of income allowed teenagers unprecedented freedom from familial restraints and societal mores. As the first purely consumer market, youth culture relied heavily on the purchasing and playback of music to express itself and create identity. Young listeners would take apart songs, transcribing lyrics and music and playing the songs themselves. The resulting rock and roll music of the 1950s was the most dramatic singular youth culture movement in history, cutting across class lines.

Muzak was apprehended through distraction whereas rock and roll was the subject of constant, engaged attention. This marked a schism. Whereas rock and roll became increasingly abrasive and strove for shock value, Muzak desired not to be heard. Unlike rock, popular with young people but hated by their elders, by the early 1950s Muzak consciously eliminated genres that were perceived as objectionable.

Architectural gestures that signal "individuality," such as those of Art Deco, Postmodernism, or Deconstructivism, require difference or shock-value in order to be effective. None of these gestures can be sustained indefinitely. Muzak lasted much longer than any twentieth century architectural movement precisely because it is neither static nor physical.

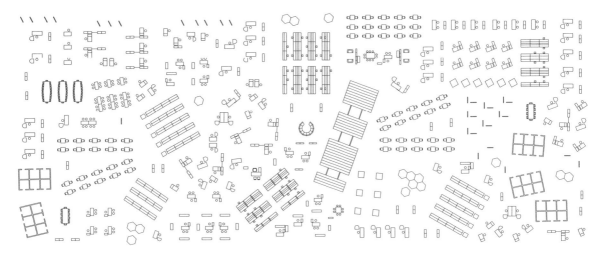

Theodor W. Adorno may well have outlined the program for postwar Muzak in his 1938 "On the Fetish-Character in Music and the Regression of Listening" when he states that since contemporary music is "perceived purely as background," it no longer has anything to do with taste: "To like it is almost the same as to recognize it." In a world of completely identical choices, recognition itself has become impossible. Preference, Adorno suggests, "depends merely on biographical details or on the situation in which things are heard." Adorno contends that active listening is at odds with contemporary music as it would reveal the banality of its arrangement. Instead, of attention, Adorno suggests, contemporary music is based on the mindless repetition of certain material and performers.

Muzak Enables the Culture of Horizontality

→ Like air-conditioning and fluorescent lighting, Muzak originally emerged as an acclimatization technology for the extreme environment of the skyscraper. Along with these technologies, it allowed vast, horizontal interior spaces, previously useable only for warehouses, to become inhabitable. The lower costs of building these new, flat structures in less expensive suburban locations, and the growing efficiency of the same data communication technologies that Muzak itself employed, soon made tall buildings obsolete.

The development of cybernetic theories after the war transformed management structures and capitalized on this new horizontality, making the office floor a source for innovation and positive change. Having learned from the Hawthorne Effect, managers no longer acted as overseers trying to keep employees from wasting time and becoming distracted from their tasks and instead encouraged employees to take on greater responsibility for themselves and their own position within the corporation. In order for employees to share information and expertise, social interaction became crucial and open environments replaced closed offices and executive floors. Large interiors became the stage where greater freedom of communication could be facilitated. In particular, the open plans and horizontal methods of organization developed by proponents of Büro Landschaft became a major aspect of both late modern architecture and management strategy.

Open plans eliminated walls completely or replaced them with partitions to allow for greater flexibility in programme and increased interaction among employees. This openness, however, also enables the unimpeded circulation of unpleasant background noise as well, including the distracting sounds of office machines, ventilation systems, coworkers, and exterior traffic. Muzak masks these background sounds, helping employees and customers focus on messages and sounds that matter while adding a layer of sensory engagement to an otherwise blank architecture. Beyond its ability to deliver cybernetic efficiency, horizontality destroys skyscrapers and kills cities. It makes possible a more fluid and responsive corporate structure, better able to respond to changing economic conditions. The lack of hierarchy and fluidity of the horizontal corporation are the very basis of contemporary society. Muzak's ability to structure an environment invisibly becomes a model for the Post-Fordist corporation.

Audio Architecture → During the 1960s, Muzak began to shift its attention, calling itself "environmental," thereby acting as a sensory stimulant adding a coloration to a space. Two decades later, then-owner Teleprompter sold Muzak to Westinghouse. The new management immediately updated the library, bringing Muzak to the foreground for the first time, playing original songs, not reorchestrated renditions. Muzak even allowed symbolism. To commemorate the return of the hostages from Iran, it played "God Bless America" several times a day.

Muzak now faces individuals with a changed sensorium. The constant flow of changes across society has made us less responsive to any particular change. Research shows that over time, our sensorium has grown more able to tolerate the shock of the new. Once shocking, both skyscrapers and sprawl have become everyday. This condition is also evidenced by changes in our relationship to music. While Elvis was radical in the 50's, he is background today. The speed with which we assimilate newness in musical culture has increased greatly over the last twenty years. Played over and over, "God Save the Queen" and "Like A Virgin" have become tunes we hum along with absent-mindedly, their messages sublimated. These popular hits work the same way that Muzak's earlier instrumentals did, acting as a stimulating but blank texture within the empty spaces of work and consumption.

When present, emotion becomes sublimated into affect that can be turned on and off at will. Violently rejecting the hippie ethic of free love and peace to the world, punk rock was the last musical or cultural movement that presented an alternative emotion. By the late 1970s, New Wave attempted to strip out emotion. Thus, while John Lennon's 1970 "Plastic Ono Band" was a raw wound, informed by Arthur Yanov's Primal Scream Therapy which sought to break through the veneer of rationalism that modern Fordism created through the aural expression of accumulated pain, in contrast, Tears for Fears's 1983 "The Hurting" addressed the same theme, but now via the nearly inflectionless lines of a synthepop dance song: "Shout, shout/Let it all out./These are the things I can do without./Come on./I'm talking to you./So come on." Ten years later, the commercial acceptance of Kurt Cobain points out how all resistance, sadness, and pain can be experienced as affect today. With Nirvana, alienation was no longer a matter of struggle, but rather could be accepted as a mood or intensity. Even prior to Cobain's death in 1994, Muzak had created an instrumental version of "Smells Like Teen Spirit." Cobain's inheritance is "Emo

Rock," which reduces emotion itself to a genre. No longer does music have to be as uninflected as New Wave. Now it can mime emotion, and we can be comforted knowing it is just an affect we can plug in and out of at will throughout the course of the day.

Always ahead of the curve, by the 1980's, Muzak abandoned the Stimulus Progression in favor of "Audio Architecture." At this point, the amount of stimulation received in the daily environment far exceeded any ability of the engineers at Muzak to modulate such forces. Over-stimulated, individuals can no longer be affected by increases in data alone. Muzak's programmers no longer style themselves as engineers or scientists. Instead they harness this excess of data to become "Audio Architects," a term that indicates not only that they construct environments, but that Muzak is as much art as science.

The sensorial overload of contemporary culture means that even original songs are no longer distracting. Today most of Muzak's channels broadcast originals, not reorchestrated versions. The result is that Muzak's audio programming has become even more invisible: if the music is audible, its source is no longer discernable.

The culture industries have made it possible for even the most wild and subversive content to be consumed by everyone. With repeated airplay, song lyrics lose their meaning, turning all music into a background of moods without emotional depth. Today, in a radically segmented demographic market, Muzak's customers can choose from a variety of programs that include all forms of music, picking the channels and moods most appropriate to their audience's needs, and can request custom selections designed to enhance their unique brand personality.

For the post-Fordist marketplace, Muzak addresses its audience's emotions, creating moods rather than seeking to manipulate attention. Muzak employs the technique of "Atmospherics" to create a distinct ambient audio environment for a particular retail environment. Through a careful choice of music, together with appropriate selections of colors, furniture, and accessories, a store can conjure the image of an entire lifestyle.

Inside a store, Muzak's cozy, ordered atmospherics offer a contrast to the chaos outside and stimulate the consumer's desire to purchase. Disoriented by noise, the proliferation of signs, and the emptiness and hustle that occurs within the vastness of either the mall or the contemporary city, the individual enters a store seeking solace and emotional comfort among a clearly ordered set of goods and experiences.

Atmospherics also solve an earlier problem that Muzak faced in stores and restaurants. Directed at transient occupants of a space, the old public-area Muzak channel had a shorter programming cycle, thereby irritating workers who had to be in the space for the entire day. In contrast, Atmospherics aim at a culture that unites workers and shoppers in a total environment.

Within the workplace, Muzak not only helps stimulate employees so that they produce more; Atmospherics form a corporate culture that helps ensure group hegemony and shared cultural references among radically different individuals. With Muzak, the ultimate product of the retail or corporate space becomes consumers and workers themselves.

The transition from the Stimulus Progression to Atmospherics echoes the shift from Fordism to Post-Fordism. The Stimulus Progression was a manifestation of the Fordist plan: it was temporal, linear, and directed at the individual, who would use it to fine-tune his or her own self. The Stimulus Progression was primarily, although not exclusively, about production. In contrast, Atmospherics are spatial, nonlinear, and self-contained. Atmospherics replace the Stimulus Progression with Quantum Modulation, which does not vary in intensity or mood. On the contrary, under Quantum Modulation, songs are numerically indexed according to criteria such as tempo, color (light or dark) rhythm, popularity and so on, to ensure that the same intensity can be maintained even as the music appears to have changed. Atmospherics address individuals as they traverse different ambiences throughout their everyday

lives. Unlike the relatively simple goals of the Stimulus Progression, Atmospherics propose that work is a form of consumption and that consumption is a form of work.

The Background Condition and the Human Chameleon → Fordist modernism understood that inserting the individual into a larger, overarching plan – be it for a city or a corporation – would appear to give a logical rationale to the process of mass industrialization while providing a theological relief from the uncertainties of modernity, creating a sort of Hawthorne Effect in the public realm. If initially the plan forced individuals to look inward and discipline themselves, the need for constant adjustment and better guidance led Fordist modernism to more explicitly direct individuals from outside. Through the Stimulus Progression, Muzak was an early form of such human programming. Turning to the background condition instead of plans is a more contemporary approach that does away with the need to guide individuals directly.

For the contemporary world the plan, which addresses the individual as individual, is too direct. We do not mean to suggest that Althusser's idea that ideology interpellates the individual was wrong, only that individuals are increasingly dissolving and that interpellation is the last thing that power needs. On the contrary, both plan and ideology are obsolete. Turning to the background condition instead is a more contemporary approach that does away with the need to guide individuals directly.

In "Mimicry and Legendary Psychasthenia," Roger Caillois observes how the process of mimicry amongst animals and insects is not so much a defensive measure as an overwhelming drive. The Phyllia, for example, looks so much like a leaf that it is prone to eating its own kind. Mimicry is not necessary for many insects, which have other defenses or are otherwise inedible. Instead, Caillois observes what he calls an "instinct of renunciation" that leads creatures to a reduced form of existence in which the organism can lose its distinction from the world and consciousness and feeling can cease. Caillois points out that in our contemporary world, space is far more complex. The subject is undermined within these spaces from the start.

With the Stimulus Progression abandoned for Atmospherics and the plan replaced by the background, the individual becomes a human chameleon, lacking either strong sense of self or a guiding plan, but instead constantly looking outward for social cues, seeking an appropriate background condition to settle upon so as to comfortably lose distinction from the world. Today, difference itself has attained its own level of banality and acceptance. The media machine ritualistically admonishes us to "Be Different," to "Be Yourself," to the point that we cannot understand what is genuine difference and what is contrived for the sake of appearance. Such difference for its own sake is akin to Internet porn: a random repetition of images, each meant to arouse and titillate more than the others. Although in the early twentieth century the individual still feared reification, or being turned into a thing by the Fordist system, the human chameleon finds that identifying with the system of objects or images is easy. The human chameleon seeks cues from things as well as from other beings. If not a Mies Barcelona chair or Karim Rashid Orgy sofa, then perhaps a wicker loveseat from Pier 1 Imports will do.

Unable to find progress or direction, the human chameleon follows Freud's Pleasure Principle, seeking to blend into its surroundings but, when that gets to be too much, breaks with them and seeks out a new environment to identify with. This can happen at various scales. We can choose our citizenship, our religion, our career, our sexual practices, even our gender. We can identify with our diverse friends, family members, ad models, television actors, serial killers, cartoon characters, and Internet avatars at will. We find pleasure in the process of identification as we see others with the same desires we have. We are less and less distinct individuals and more and more surfers on a wave of mass subjectivities held by many people all at once. In order to function within the contemporary city, we have all become human chameleons without a sense of home. Beyond merely moving from place to place, we move from self to self according to the social conditions we find ourselves in.

Architecture is Muzak → As the most visible products of society that literally shape our environment, buildings provide social cues. Architecture structures group relationships by articulating moods and milieus within the ubiquitous horizontality of the contemporary urban realm. In the continuous construction of the postmetropolitan realm, architecture now takes on the same role that Muzak played within the office block: it adds color to our lives. Sometimes it is fast, sometimes it is slow. On rare occasions, it is engaging; more often it is banal and background.

Individual works of architecture now become examples of Atmospherics: a relationship between emotional forms whereby a sense of movement, from effect to effect, is generated for the multitude to experience. Stimulus Progression is replaced by Quantum Modulation. We no longer change to create growth and make progress, but to make one day progress differently from the others. The variation of stimuli within the built environment helps us to remain engaged with the world, by adjusting to constant change.

Architecture first fully realizes its potential with the mirror glass curtain wall building, developed in the 1970s. The reflections of the structure's surroundings in the surface creates a facade of infinite variation while the disappearance of clearly defined window openings replaces the bourgeois notion of the individual with a limitless free space. Transparency is replaced not with opacity, but with the image of the city itself in perpetual flux.

Just as Muzak ordered the background condition of the late modern office building, Muzak now makes possible the contemporary condition in which the city itself becomes a background condition, rendering the delirious vertical expressiveness of the skyscraper and the signature object obsolete. Just as contemporary culture can absorb any content, the contemporary urban realm is capable of absorbing any amount of difference. And just as the horizontal office building made the skyscraper obsolete, new telecommunications technology – cell phones, email, and instant messaging – have made the horizontal world of office landscape obsolete in turn. Physical boundaries no longer impede communication and open space no longer enables it.

Instead, office plans merely become infill, endlessly adapting to real estate footprints. Architecture, which had previously been a marker of difference, is similarly reduced to a background condition. But architecture does not merely go away as it recedes into the background condition of the city; instead it is transformed, as every gesture and emotion produced through architectural form becomes a variation along a stimulus progression deployed throughout the city. Minimalism, the Blob, and the Spanish Revival seamlessly coexist in the city without qualities.In the absence of real public spaces and collective icons, empty visual markers are developed to signify the presence of culture within a city. A tacit agreement has been reached between developers and urban planners: cutting edge concert halls and museums, McMansions, historic districts and limitless sprawl co-exist merrily in the contemporary city. This urban condition makes possible the necessary illusion that individuation and autonomy remain options even as society continues to move toward an immaterial culture. Recent advertisements for downtown living verify this, suggesting that if one lives high up enough, one can dispense with curtains and clothes. According to the ad copy, better sex and greater freedom of expression are made possible against the anonymous background of the city. Skyscrapers retain their importance not for their forms or interiors, but for the vertical distance they create, whereby occupants can see the city as a background view.

As the lessons of industrial psychology and Muzak suggest, even meaningless change and variation makes us feel like someone or something is responding to us, filling the deadly silence of the city with a form of simulated interaction.

Selected References

Archizoom, "No-Stop City. Residential Parkings. Climatic Universal Sistem," *Domus* 496, March 1971, 49-55.
Roger Callois, "Mimicry and Legendary Psychasthenia," *October* 31 (Winter, 1984), 16-32.
Paul Wilson Clark, *Major George Owen Squier: Military Scientist*, Ph. D. dissertation, Case Western Reserve University, 1974.
Gilles Deleuze, "Postscript on Control Societies," *Negotiations: 1972-1990*, trans. Martin Joughin (New York: Columbia University Press, 1990), pp. 177-182.
Evan Eisenberg, *The Recording Angel: Explorations in Phonography* (New York: McGraw-Hill, 1987).
Anthony Haden-Guest, *The Paradise Program; Travels through Muzak, Hilton, Coca-Cola, Texaco, Walt Disney, and Other World Empires* (New York: W. Morrow, 1973).
Jane Hulting, *Muzak: A Study in Sonic Ideology*, Thesis M A in Communication, Annenberg School of Communications University of Pennsylvania, 1988.
Jerri Ann Husch, *Music of the Workplace: A Study of Muzak Culture*, Dissertation. University of Massachusetts, 1984.
Friedrich A. Kittler, *Gramophone, Film, Typewriter* (Stanford, Calif.: Stanford University Press, 1999).
Joseph Lanza, *Elevator Music: A Surreal History of Muzak, Easy-Listening, and Other Moodsong* (New York: St. Martin's Press, 1994).
Jonathan Sterne, *The Audible Past: Cultural Origins of Sound Reproduction* (Durham: Duke University Press, 2003).

verb SoundLab is a small room where one can experience the acoustic character of any space, built or unbuilt, of any width, height, shape or material. The lab, designed by Arup Acoustics, generates an accurate acoustic preview that increases the malleability of sound and allows for a level of precision previously unattainable with more empirical acoustic data. SoundLab is the achievement of acoustic effects modeled on the computer in physical space – close your eyes and you're inside a concert hall. No longer virtual reality, but the making real of the virtual.

**SoundLab
Arup Acoustics**

What is SoundLab? → SoundLab allows you to experience the sound of existing spaces or predict the sound of spaces that are yet to be realized. It uses a process called "Auralization" to create 3d renderings of sound – the aural equivalent of 3d visual renderings produced by architects and designers.

The SoundLab itself is an acoustically neutral space, resembling a recording studio. The dimensions are specifically chosen for their acoustic quality. The walls and ceiling are lined with sound absorbing materials so there are no sound reflections in the room. This creates the perfect environment for listening to musical sounds and specifically identifying and understanding the acoustical nuances of spaces. The space is also isolated from surrounding spaces with heavy wall, floor and ceiling constructions to provide the listener with a completely controlled listening environment.

In the room there are 12 loudspeakers arranged according to a principle known as ambisonics. These loudspeakers create a sphere of sound in the room. When you are seated in the center of the space you are in the "sweet spot".

At this sweet spot, these loudspeakers can be used to reproduce the exact direction, location and strength of individual sound reflections, from any space, regardless of size. Sound reflections in a large concert hall are reproduced in the SoundLab environment. In order to validate and calibrate the accuracy of SoundLab, we measured over 60 prestigious concert halls around the world and have conducted over 15 years of research in building acoustics. By comparing real measurements in real spaces to computer models of the same spaces, we have been able to accurately calibrate the system to ensure that what is produced is as close as possible to the real environment and hence apply the design process to new buildings.

SoundLab is a small isolated anechoic room with twelve loudspeakers and a screen.

A 3-D ambiasonic auralization and visualization of a space even before it has been constructed.

Data → Specific information is required in order to create the auralizations in the SoundLab. The most important of these is the "Impulse Response" of the space, which effectively provides it with a unique acoustic signature. We use a source sound called an "impulse," a short, sharp sound similar to a gun shot. We play it through an omnidirectional loudspeaker – one that sends equal energy in all directions, to stimulate sound reflections from as many room surfaces as possible. This reflection sequence is captured using a 3D SoundField microphone, a special microphone that allows us to capture and individually analyze reflection information in the X (front-to-back), Y (side-to-side), Z (floor-to-ceiling) and W (simultaneous X, Y, Z) axes. We can also produce acoustical computer models of spaces. These are 3d models of the space that contain specific data regarding the room surfaces – how much sound they reflect, absorb and diffuse (scatter). In the same way as a real room, the model can allow us to determine the impulse response with all the details of direction, timing and strength.

The next stage is to determine what is being listened to in the space. This can be music (classical, jazz, pop, etc), speech, or ambient sounds of people conducting other activities. However, in order to produce the auralizations these sounds need to be recorded anechoically – in a room that has no sound reflections in it at all.

Finally, these two components, the anechoic sound and the impulse response (which gives the room a reflection sequence), are combined through a complex mathematical process known as convolution. What you finally hear is a combination of the two.

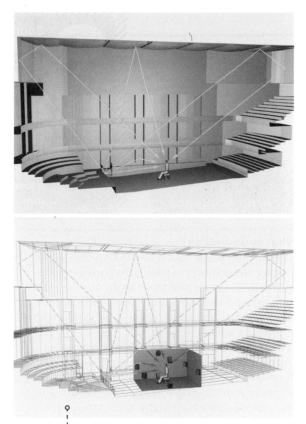

The Principle of Auralization – the computer model of the concert hall is used to calculate the transfer function between source and receiver, which is then multiplied with anechoic music to produce the auralization of the hall.

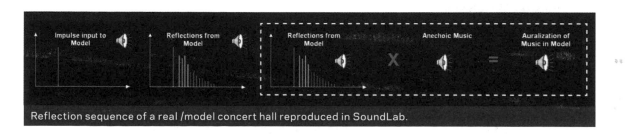

Reflection sequence of a real /model concert hall reproduced in SoundLab.

Objectives and Expectations → The objective of SoundLab is to provide a process and an environment in which we can actually listen to the spaces we are designing and use listening as a way of benchmarking, improving and optimizing designs.

The science of acoustics has been undergoing a constant progression since the mid-1940's when most research had been applied to war time activity, radar, sonar and the like. Since then, the science of acoustics has been refined and developed in relation to how it can be used to better improve conditions in buildings, control noise in the environment, control noise from equipment (everything from oil rigs to the household vacuum cleaner), etc. Until SoundLab, one aspect has remained constant; the advice given by acoustic consultants to clients, architects or designers was empirical in nature. Acoustics was quantified in numbers and consultants would use this information to then advise the designers on what they should do to improve the acoustics. The main problem with the "old way" is that either the designer needs to put his full trust in the acoustician, or a somewhat adversarial relationship develops with the designer not being able to tangibly understand why aspects of a design need to change.

There are also, of course, many examples of buildings, even those specifically designed for music, which turn out to have bad acoustics. Often, the designer and his consultant may have followed well-known, successful benchmark designs, but make what appear to have been small deviations to geometry or materials that in fact fundamentally alter the acoustics.

The two main aims of SoundLab were to:
1 → Have a tool to help us learn more and design better through listening.
2 → Provide an environment in which to work proactively with clients and architects through listening to how their spaces sound.

In both of these respects the SoundLab has surpassed our expectations. It has completely changed the way in which we conduct our work. Rather than relying on empirical calculations and analysis we now listen to all the spaces we design. We can analyze every nuance of sound, manipulate and experiment with geometry and the optimization of materials.

We were most intrigued as to how our clients would find using the SoundLab, particularly architects who are more attuned to the visual rather than the aural. Interestingly, many people come to the lab and open with a comment such as "I haven't got great hearing" or "I'm not particularly good at listening," perhaps skeptical that they will be able to hear differences in sounds. They come away with a sense of elation, initially because they really can hear the differences, but perhaps most importantly, they see how SoundLab can be used proactively in the design process to make it better.

Changes → The ways in which SoundLab is impacting the design process are already clear to see. Clients and designers now meet with us at a much earlier stage of the design process in order to work on acoustics as a fundamental aspect of their design.

It allows us to quickly establish and provide a common knowledge base of how different spaces sound and how this is related to project goals. Basic acoustical concepts are understood much more quickly, as well as the reasons behind fundamental aspects of the acoustician's advice. This significantly speeds up the early design process for this design discipline. For certain building types it reinforces the need for particular shape, form or materials. But significantly, in other cases, it shows that there can be departures from the norm without significant impact on the acoustics, thus liberating the designer to experiment with geometry and materials in new and exciting ways, while allowing the client to remain confident that a successful result will be achieved.

Also, very importantly, acoustic design will have cost implications. Allowing clients to subjectively assess the performance of any aspect of their building through listening, means they can make judgments on where they feel the money is best spent.

User → Our work as acoustic consultants is wide-ranging, from concert halls to commercial offices, opera houses to airports, subway stations to schools, residential buildings to railways and everything in between. SoundLab has had an impact on every part of our business.

In the case of concert hall design, for example, we can play the same piece of music and move from hall to hall around the world and compare this to a new design. This aspect of the lab has helped our understanding of spaces and helped us work much more proactively with clients and architects to get the sound they want for their new halls.

Arup Acoustics had a number of auditorium design projects underway and under construction at the time that SoundLab was perfected. Although the lab was not used to design them, it was used as a means to assess their performance while under construction. One example is **The Sage Gateshead Concert Hall**, which opened in December 2004 and was designed by Arup Acoustics in conjunction with Foster and Partners. The 1800-seat hall has a sophisticated system of moving ceiling panels and curtains that allow the room acoustics to be changed depending on event type. SoundLab was used to analyze and listen to different room configurations in advance of the building completion and to conduct tests with real musicians. It allowed us to select what we believed to be optimum settings for each event type and quickly react with options following comments from the musicians. It was an exceptional method of speeding up the process of fine-tuning a concert hall before opening to the public.

For subway stations, airports and sports stadiums, there is an important balance to be struck between control of acoustics, speech intelligibility of the sound system, and noise from ventilation and other building equipment. SoundLab allows us to listen to all of these aspects independently and together. Fundamentally this allows us to optimize the design of the space and minimize the expenditure on materials or systems related to acoustics.

Other Applications → Noise from sources such as roads, railways, planes, helicopters, building equipment, etc. affect almost every aspect of our lives, regardless of whether we live in areas that are urban, suburban or rural. We can use SoundLab to assess noise from all of these sources and determine mitigation options. Forexample, take the design of a new residential building close to a railway. The building needs to be designed to control vibration and noise from the railway coming into the building. SoundLab can be used to determine the optimum performance of the building façade to limit noise ingress to an appropriate level. This helps the architect, structural engineer, and façade engineer in designing the façade to make it as light and cost effective as possible for the client. We can determine whether the building structure needs to be isolated from the railway vibration and assess different structural options. We can work out what the internal walls and floors need to be to appropriately limit noise transfer from one space to another. The same technique can be used to assess the introduction of a new road, railway or airport near residential communities and determine how to mitigate noise impacts. To take another example, in education buildings it is of paramount importance that students can hear and understand the teacher. Speech intelligibility is crucial, and understanding how to achieve optimum acoustical conditions is crucial in the design process.

As stated by Andrew Blum in *The New York Times*, "SoundLab will transform acoustics design in the same way three-dimensional computer animations have transformed visual design."

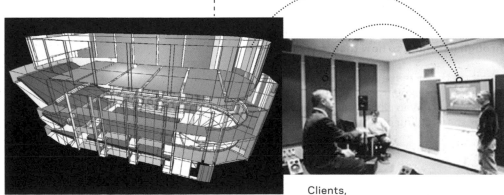

Sage Gateshead Concert Hall

Clients,
architects,
engineers,
musicians,
etc...

Sound visualization 3-D graphic animation showing sound propagation

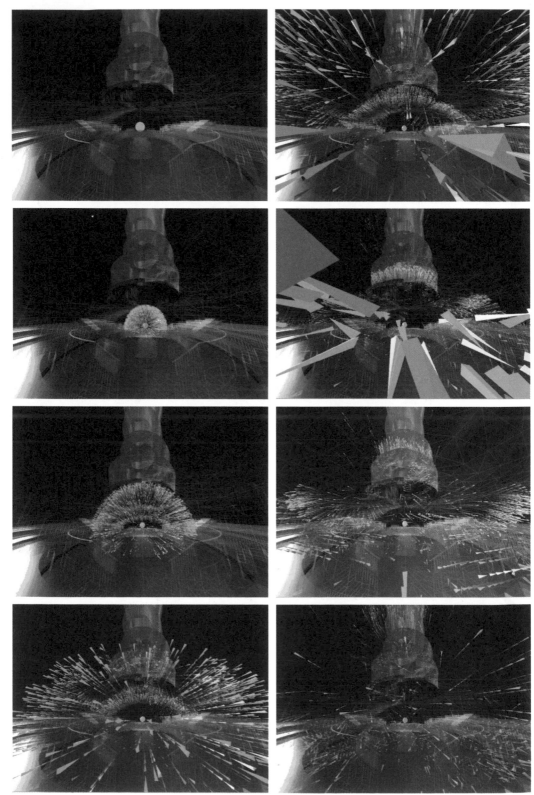

How to use the SoundLab Example

Improving the Sound of Avery Fisher Hall.
Aural evaluation showed the Avery Fisher Hall lacks intimacy and reverberation. This is a demonstration of how this hall could sound after a series of proposed modifications to the design. On the Arup web page, you can listen to the acoustics by changes to the space and material modification, compared to the world's finest concert halls. ▪

http://www.arup.com/acoustics/soundlab/001_concerthall_renovation.htm

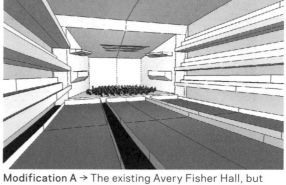

Modification A → The existing Avery Fisher Hall, but with the sound diffusing side wall finishes changed to a flat plastered surface.

Modification B → As in modification A, but with the upper balcony removed. This noticeably increase reverberation time.

Modification C → As in modification B, but with a new stage configuration. The forestage has been extended to bring the orchestra into the room, whereas the real wall of the stage recess has been moved forward to give a more intimate sound.

Modification D → As in modification C, but with new lightly upholstered seats to reduce low frequency absorption.

Modification E → As in modification D, but with a new wall added at the stall level to reduce the hall width, improving lateral reflections to improve intimacy and envelopment.

data — **Arup SoundLab** → Locations: New York, London, Hong Kong, Melbourne. **Client:** Various. **Design:** Arup Acoustics. **Floor area:** undisclosed. **Number of floors:** 1. **Structure:** n/a. **Other:** 12 Dynaudio BM5 loudspeakers. **Computers:** 2 x Dell Pentium 4, 1 x Mac G5 running AutoCAD, Rhino, CATT Acoustics, Odeon, MaxMSP, MATLAB. **Text:** Raj Patel, Arup Acoustics, New York. **Images:** Arup. **www.arup.com/acoustics**

verb

The following prototypes developed by the Décosterd & Rahm partnership, which dissolved in the end of 2004, use atmospheric conditions as building materials. Air consistency, temperature, brightness, luminosity, color... These are the physical variables that define the spatial and functional organizations of their controlled environments. Beyond the use of conventional construction materials, the manipulation of these variables determines architectural experience and affects the user through the five senses – pushing these boundaries to include even negative effects, like chambers that cannot be entered without destroying the body. The selection of projects that follow has been compiled with Philippe Rahm, who now runs an office independently.

See www.philipperahm.com

Décosterd & Rahm,
Hormonorium,
Swiss Pavilion
8th Venice Architecture Biennale, 2002
Photo : Niklaus Stauss, Zurich

Invisible Architecture / Philippe Rahm

Today, globalization and climatic disturbance – two important mutations of the beginning of the 21st century – have engendered a deep transformation of the notions of space and time. Architectural space is no longer defined in terms of day and night, local and far, hot or cold, light or dark, but in a sort of global and permanent climatic continuum. There is the same light, average temperature and constant level of humidity everywhere. Architecture deploys itself in a henceforth universal space, projecting without discontinuity an eternal continuous present that is invariable, everywhere the same, always there. The continuum creates spatiality and temporality extending beyond biological cycles, without sleep or season, outside of astronomical and climatic rhythms, without night or winter, without rain or chill. Information is instantaneous, connections simultaneous, and the communications network is global, uninterrupted. Here and now, but also over there and tomorrow, all meteorological variables have been stabilized to an average of shared comfort: somewhere around 21° Celsius, relative humidity at 50%, light intensity at 2000 lux – a beautiful spring day in Paris that we have decided to repeat infinitely, all over the world.

In this eternal climatic homogeneity, architecture is the instrument that enables us to articulate this continuum, to create fault-lines, ruptures, and fog. Making certain climates swell punctually or momentarily, naturalizing a context or contrarily distancing it even more: creating moments, generating meteorologies, projecting seasons and times, spatializing functions, shortening or amplifying distances, diminishing the length of the day or creating an endless night, here and there, out of time and space. Going backwards, from winter to summer. Working through climatic disturbance, desynchronization, making form appear and modifying it through seasonal shifts, projecting through thermo-periodization, through dormancy or vernalization. Going back several hours, several months, a season, finding this moment of comfort that we lost as the year advanced, going back from winter to fall, from night to afternoon. Architecture as constructed temporalities.

Curatorial statement of *Invisible Architecture*, an exhibition at the Centre Culturel Suisse, Paris (2005). With projects by Bauart / cero9 / Dominique Gonzalez-Foerster / Diller Scofidio + Renfro / fabric | ch / Christelle Lheureux **www.ccsparis.com**

Absinth' Air®
Décosterd & Rahm

20°C

'By a singular ambiguity, by a kind of transposition or
intellectual misunderstanding, you will feel yourself evaporating,
and you will attribute to your pipe the strange ability to smoke you.'
Charles Baudelaire, *Les paradis artificiels*

data

Centre Culturel Suisse, Paris
http://www.ccsparis.com/projets/mursollaici/index.html
From 18 January to 30 March 2003
Décosterd & Rahm, associés (Philippe Rahm, Jean-Gilles Décosterd, Sébastien Chevance).
With technical support from:
Thierry Dutheil, ETE consultant engineer (Lausanne) and Yves Kübler, distiller (Môtiers)
Original design of the Absinth'Air® flyer: Fabien Verschaere, Galerie Michel Rein, Paris.

The outfitting that we proposed for the Centre Culturel Suisse in Paris developed from a study of modern climitization techniques and air conditioning. The project is an immediate response to the physical need to heat and ventilate the Centre Culturel Suisse by creating a material and cultural dependency between France and Switzerland. Absinth' Air® opens up the qualification of the space to the chemical influences of inanimate and vegetable substances on mood and behavior. Like a fantasy of Jules Verne's 'Doctor Ox', Absinth' Air® is a contemporary reproduction of the old and perverse late-19th-century alliance between drunkenness and creativity, internal physiological stimulation and artistic expression, thujone (the main ingredient in absinthe) and poetry. The project focuses on the physical link between the Val-de-Travers and Paris: the psychotropic influence of the Neuchâteloise cultures of absinthe and fennel on the Parisian Bohemia, a geographical and chemical link whose forms are deployed first in the space and subsequently in the intestines, the lungs, the brain. No word is heard, no form is seen. Only alimentary particles and active principles are absorbed: we inhale and retain only traces, symptoms, absinthe iris...
Absinth' Air® is an ambient prosthesis that plugs into the intake vent of the air-conditioning system. At the Centre Culturel Suisse, this apparatus is affixed to an external ventilation grille. It functions on the hookah principle by passing fresh air from the exterior through a volume of liquid absinthe, distilled in the Val-de-Travers, charging the air with alcohol and the scent of absinthe.
This absinthe-conditioned air is then heated to 20° C before being pumped into the Centre's exhibition rooms. What the visitors receive from our intervention will be perceptible in terms of vapor, exhalation, perfume, smell, breath, and drunkenness.

Air conditioning = heavy drinking

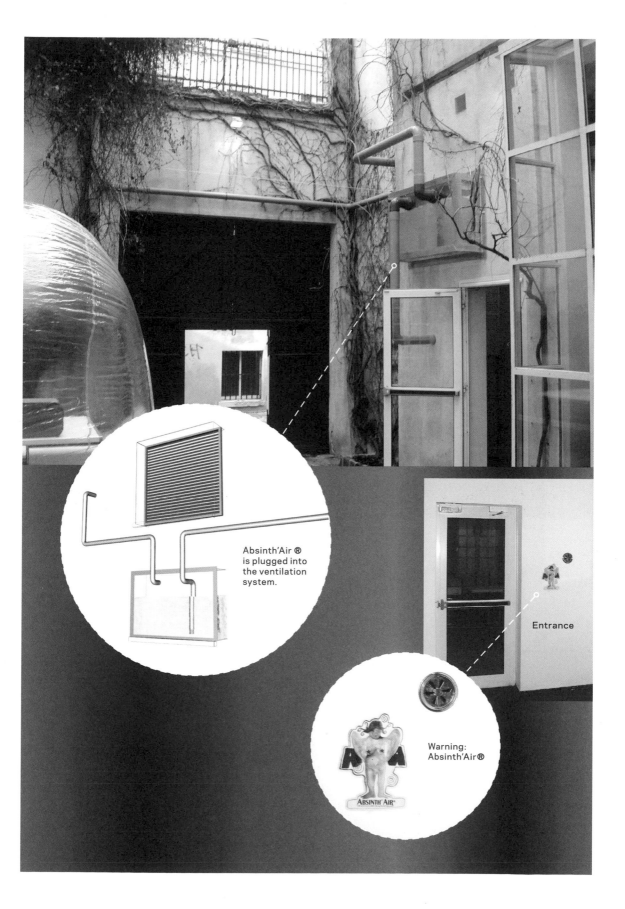

Absinth'Air ®
is plugged into
the ventilation
system.

Entrance

Warning:
Absinth'Air®

Lucy Mackintosh Contemporary Art Gallery
Décosterd & Rahm

16-30°C

data

Clients: Lucy Mackintosh and Cyril Veillon
Décosterd & Rahm, associés
Collaborator: Jérôme Jacqmin
Project: 2004

The existing volume is a simple empty space of 8 m x 35 m x 3 m. The plan is to create a gallery exhibiting contemporary art, composed of a receiving desk, library and archives, with the majority of the space dedicated as a large exhibition area.

Our proposal is to define the space through differing degrees of heat. Certain areas of the space are influenced by temperature to create different zones for different functions: working and sitting at 21°C, touring the show at 19°C, storing artworks at 16°C. The space will be empty and completely open, without partitions.

A tubular network of warm and cold water runs through the space, compressed in some zones and expanded in others, offering a variety of conditions, spaces and temperatures. The network functions as a circuit of warm water in winter and of cold water during the summer. Through convection, the surrounding air is either warmed or cooled. The network is warmer the closer one is to it, and becomes progressively cooler as one moves further away.

This architecture is not tectonic, but thermic in nature: to impart form to the space via radiation, to divide by conduction and plan through convection. During winter, the network will have a conditioning range of 21°C to 16°C, and in summer, 30°C to 18°C. The circuit contracts in order to concentrate its heating capacity and touches the floor, wall and ceiling. This network also forms a table surface, a bench and a bar, generating the space around it according to its needs. The network neither contains nor encloses.

Temperature = functional specialization

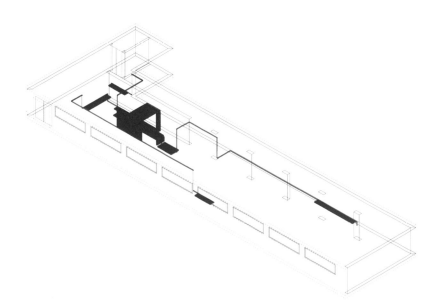

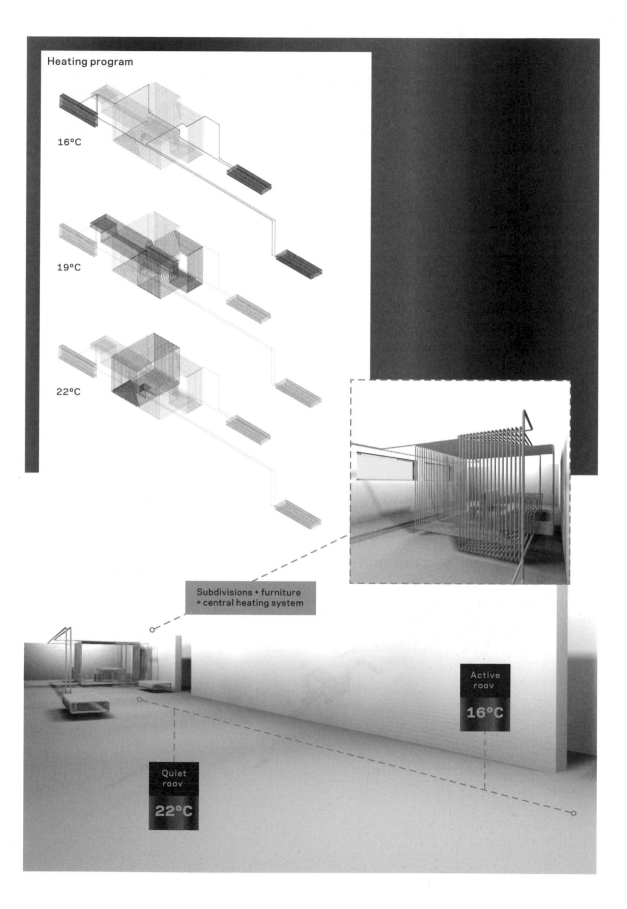

Heating program

16°C

19°C

22°C

Subdivisions + furniture
= central heating system

Active roov

16°C

Quiet roov

22°C

data

Exhibition "Nano", curated by Laurence Dreyfus
Paris, 2003
Décosterd & Rahm, associés
(Philippe Rahm, Jean-Gilles Décosterd, Sébastien Chevance)

In the spectrum between 670 and 254 nanometers we constructed a series of spaces that follow each other in a linear manner, from largest to smallest, from visible to invisible, from inhabitable to uninhabitable. This progression occurs along a course in which space reduces itself from a single unit into ever simpler and smaller components. We arranged a gradual reduction of white light together with a macroscopic reduction of space. The first and largest chamber is flooded with white light comprised of superimposed red, green and violet – the entire visible light spectrum from 400 to 670 nanometers. In the second chamber, which is more narrow and squat, we removed the red, creating a yellow atmosphere lit with wavelengths between 400 and 550 nanometers. In the third chamber, which is the height of an average man, we eliminated wavelengths corresponding to green: the only remaining light is blue-violet, falling between 400 and 500 nanometers. We must kneel in order to enter the fourth room. Here we descend into shorter wavelengths and abandon visible light, left with only the ultraviolet. This fourth chamber is flooded with UV-A waves at 360 nanometers, a black light that tans the skin with vitamin D. The fifth and last chamber is inaccessible: with a height of only 40 cm, we can only insert our heads. A UV-C germicide and ozone-creating lamp is set up at the back of the room to emit 254-nanometer electromagnetic rays that destroy viruses and bacteria while attacking other forms of life, including our own. Here the type of electromagnetic radiation makes the room uninhabitable – the limit of the infinitely small dimension where space becomes harmful, burning our skin and penetrating deeply and destructively into our bodies.

Wavelength of light = function of the room

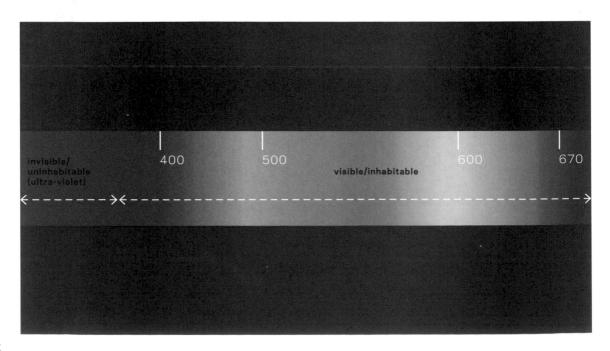

invisible/
uninhabitable
(ultra-violet)

400   500   600   670

visible/inhabitable

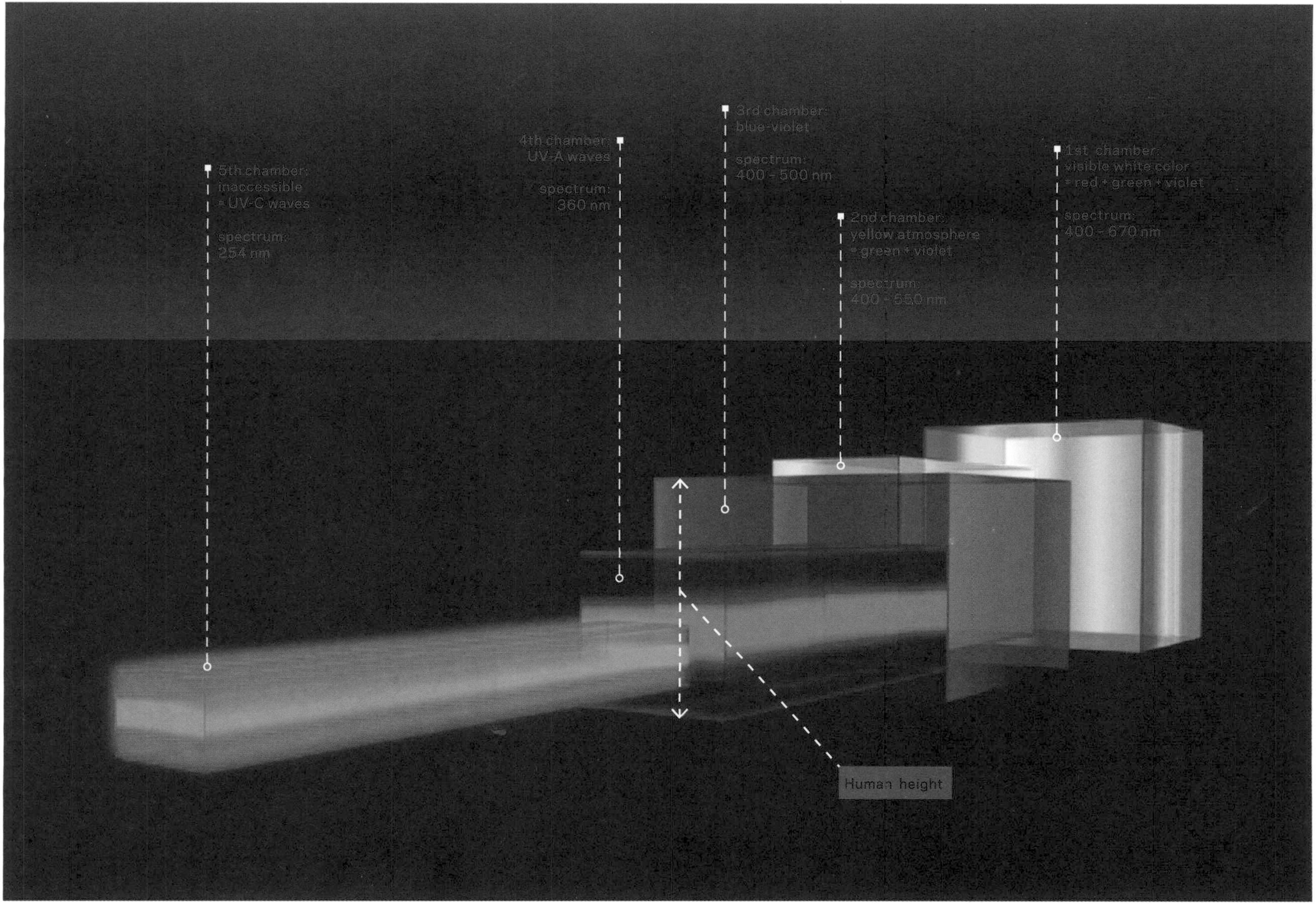

1st chamber:
visible white color
= red + green + violet
spectrum:
400 - 670 nm

2nd chamber:
yellow atmosphere
= green + violet
spectrum:
400 - 550 nm

3rd chamber:
blue-violet
spectrum:
400 - 500 nm

4th chamber:
UV-A waves
spectrum:
360 nm

5th chamber:
inaccessible
= UV-C waves
spectrum:
254 nm

Human height

Ghost Spaces Normally, architecture is understood as a universe in three dimensions. Ghost Spaces is a project of living in unknown dimensions through the amplification of the current spectrum of the sensible to reach new extents, dissimulated in the folds of time and space. Bilocation, ubiquity, channeling: through the synchronic presence of various spatial dimensions, we can draw an architecture that intersects spectrums of spaces – one room haunted by another, where a phantom of one program can appear in another.

Ghost Flat
Décosterd & Rahm

350-800 NM

data

Curators : Akiko Miyake, Nobuo Nakamura
CCA Kitakyushu, Japan, March 22 - April 30, 2004
(link: http://www.cca-kitakyushu.org)
Philippe Rahm with the participation of Marie Darrieussecq
Consultant : Professor Libero Zuppiroli, EPFL

Ghost Flat is a housing project by Philippe Rahm where the various spaces do not reside in three-dimensional space but instead take shape among the various wavelengths of the visible light spectrum. Exisiting simultaneously in the same surface, intermingling their mass and their volumes, each part of the program (bedroom, living room, bathroom) occupies a specific fraction of the electromagnetic spectrum. The bedroom materializes between 400 and 500 nanometers, the living room between 600 and 800 nanometers; the bathroom is located in the ultraviolet, between 350 and 400 nanometers.

Wavelength of light = function of the room

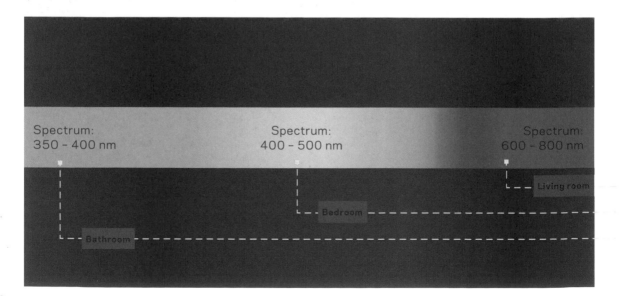

Spectrum:
350 - 400 nm

Spectrum:
400 - 500 nm

Spectrum:
600 - 800 nm

Living room

Bedroom

Bathroom

data
Curator : Marie-Ange Brayer
Frac Centre, Orléans, France, 2005
Philippe Rahm

Ghost show is a solo exhibition designed by Philippe Rahm. It presents architecture projects in three spaces at three different moments in time. Each space is defined volumetrically by the twelve edges of a virtual parallelepiped of variable size (27 m³, 36 m³ and 60 m³), one face of which is filled by printed sheets. These volumes are supported alternately on the ground, the wall or the ceiling, and each is associated with a particular color (cyan, magenta or yellow). Time intervals are defined by the emission of one fixed duration of a particular color of light (cyan, magenta or yellow) that is also associated with a video projection. 100 fluorescent lights in three colors ignite alternatively over 30 minute cycles. According to time and color, the visibility of one space dominates while the other volumes fade slightly into the general gray of the Frac Centre.

Time intervals = visibility of the space

100 fluorescent tubes in 3 colors illuminate the space, changing its visibility and shape through the concealment of different volumes.

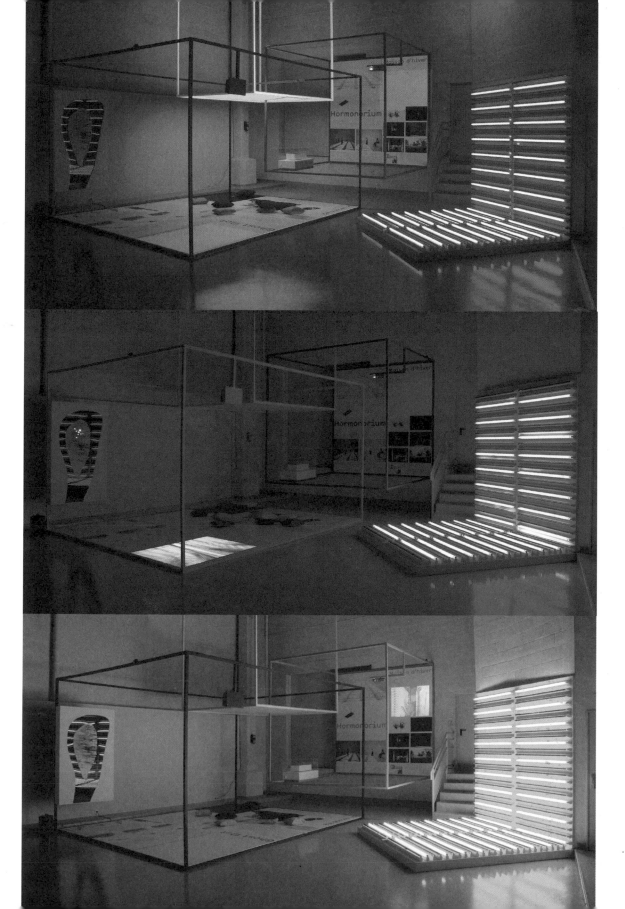

data

House in Vendée, France, for Fabrice Hybert
Design and construction : 2002 - 2006
Décosterd & Rahm, associés
Collaboration : Jérôme Jacqmin
Exhibition "L'image habitable", Version A,
Centre pour l'image contemporaine, Geneva, 2002
Collection of the Musée National d'art moderne,
CCI, Centre Georges Pompidou, Paris

20°C

This project examines the invisible modification of space through modern climate control. It aims to extend the field of architecture into the design of the invisible, of electromagnetic fields and chemical realms. Proceeding from one of the primary rationales of domestic architecture, the artifical definition of a climate inhabitable by man, we seek to define a quality that is both chemical and plastic. The house will be in the Vendée countryside, near a small river, at a distance from other dwellings. We imagine it as a winter refuge, a conditioned space that will afford protection against cold and harsh winter weather conditions. Our design intends to restore the task of designing the technical aspects of the building to specialist engineers, where heating and ventilation become architectural elements. Hence the physical material of the heating and ventilation system are not merely secondary aspects of the architecture, but become its fundamental *raison d'être*. When positioned in an outdoor temperature of 5°C, the interior of the house is climate-controlled to 20°C, with 50% humidity. If modern climate control is abstract and invisible, we propose here to interpret it as the artificial reproduction of a geographically localized, chemically determined climate. Thus, according to the desires of the occupant, the interior of the house in Vendée becomes a meridional (tropical) climate during winter. For this purpose we have developed an architecture of air, invisible but physically modified. The heating system becomes a space for the production of this air, containing not only technical apparatuses but also exotic plants, earth, microorganisms and mineral substances from distant regions where the temperature is actually 20°C with 50% humidity. Through photosynthesis and their emanations, plants will determine the chemical quality of the air, which will then be pulsed into the living space. The light in this space will be a real-time reproduction of the astronomical rhythm and light intensity characteristics of the de-localized region.

House in Vendée = Tahitian climate

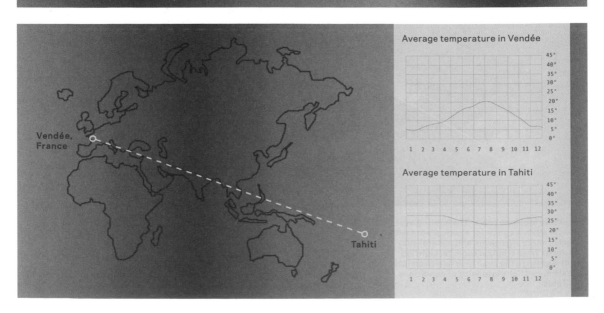

Vendée,
France

Tahiti

Average temperature in Vendée

Average temperature in Tahiti

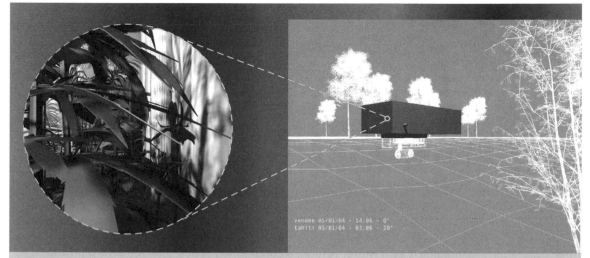

↑ Inside, 20°C and 50% humidity: a Tahitian tropical climate

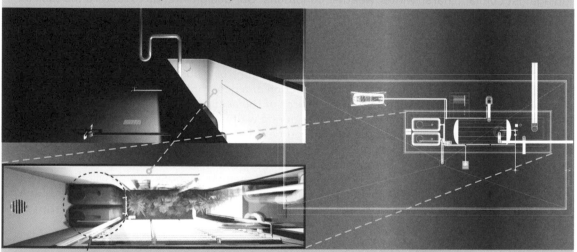

↓ Axonometric of air heating system   ↑ Heating system space

→ Living machine room: The heating system is alive, a space for exotic plants with earth, microorganisms and mineral substances from tropical regions. Lighting will duplicate the real-time astronomical rhythm and light intensity of conditions in Tahiti.

verb The final frontier in the conditioning of environmental effects. Beyond the effects of sound, temperature, luminosity and UV radiation (see Décosterd and Rahm), the sense of gravity is the most primitive and omnipresent of sensory cues, one so ubiquitous it would seem to be beyond alteration. The following three projects, by Theodore W. Hall, Umbilical Design, and ETALAB, constitute a first exploration of the potentials of gravity and weightlessness, a new science whose problems ultimately lie in the depths of the human body itself.

Theodore W. Hall
The Gravity of Architecture
The Architecture of Gravity

Gravity → Gravity imbues the space we inhabit with an inherent structure. Six directions on three axes are innately perceptible: up-down (height), left-right (breadth), and front-back (depth). The up-down axis is tied to the force of gravity – the plumb line – while the other axes are free to rotate around it. The up-down axis is called "vertical", while all possible left-right and front-back axes are called "horizontal". The anisotropic character of this space arises from the effort required to move in different directions: up and down are distinct irreversible poles, while left, right, front, and back are interchangeable simply by turning around. Thus, we conceive three principal directions – up, down, and horizontal – and three basic architectural elements – ceiling, floor, and wall. The walls, which bind the horizontal dimensions, are not inherently distinct. North, south, east, and west faces are all "walls"; none of them is a "floor" or a "ceiling", nor are "floor" and "ceiling" interchangeable. Terrestrial architecture can isolate its inhabitants from any clue to cardinal orientation, but it cannot isolate them from gravity.

Physical Effects → Humans adapt almost too well to weightlessness. From the day they enter orbit, their minds and bodies conform to the demands of the new environment. Blood and other fluids that previously pooled in the lower extremities now shift toward the torso and head, triggering a domino effect of autonomous physiological changes that include: fluid redistribution; fluid loss; electrolyte imbalances; cardiovascular changes, with an initial expansion followed by the reduction of the

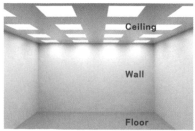

Room in terrestrial gravity

Room in artificial gravity

heart's left ventricular volume; loss of red blood cells; loss of muscle mass, as well as a reduction of slow-twitch red fiber relative to fast-twitch white fiber; loss of bone minerals and structure; hypercalcemia (excessive levels of calcium in the blood); loss of immune response; vertigo and disorientation; nausea; lethargy; head congestion with a loss of smell and taste; loss of appetite. Some of these adjustments are initially unpleasant, but within a few days the nausea subsides as the brain disregards haphazard vestibular cues and relies more on visual cues for orientation. Before long, astronauts are floating comfortably in their weightlessness realm while their muscles and bones continue to shed their now useless mass.

Trouble ensues upon the return to Earth. Muscle and bone is suddenly needed again, but what was lost over a period of weeks or months cannot be regained in minutes or seconds. If astronauts intend to return to life with gravity, they must exercise diligently to prevent their complete adaptation to weightlessness, especially in order to maintain their bones, muscles, and cardiovascular fitness.

Besides the physiological adaptations, weightlessness presents a myriad of practical problems. Activities that commonly rely on weight for traction, stability, or flow, may be simple on Earth but are difficult in weightlessness. The Skylab shower was watertight and drained by a vacuum; the astronauts plugged their noses and breathed through an air hose to avoid inhaling water droplets. Splashed or spilled water, food crumbs, dropped pencils, and other litter hang suspended in the air until settling into a corner or migrating into an air vent. Habitat designers must provide adequate padding and eliminate sharp protrusions that might injure the inhabitants. However, these engineering details and the mechanical problems pale in comparison to the medical.

Three Gravities: earth, zero, artificial → More than any other feature of the environment, gravity is a common denominator of life on Earth. If designers could provide artificial gravity in space environments, similar to the way they provide artificial lighting, heating, cooling, and ventilation, they might avoid much of the trouble that weightlessness entails.

TransHab inflatable space habitat, designed by Constance Adams, Kriss Kennedy, et al., Lockheed Martin Space Operations Company and NASA Johnson Space Center.

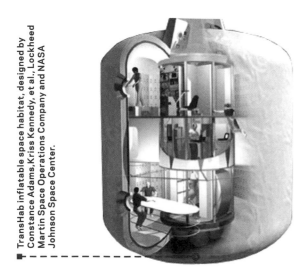

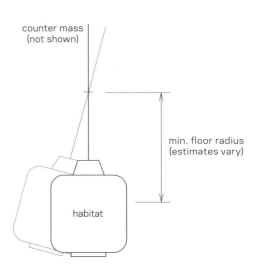

counter mass
(not shown)

min. floor radius
(estimates vary)

habitat

Astronauts feel weightless because they have no stable platform upon which to bear their weight. People on Earth feel weight not because gravity pulls them down, but because the floor pushes them up. To provide astronauts with weight, there must be an "upward" force. According to Newton's Second Law of Motion, that force will cause them to accelerate and their velocity must continually change as long as a force is applied.

If the force is aligned with the velocity, we have linear acceleration, which if sustainable, would be a near perfect substitute for natural gravity. Unfortunately, a continuous energy input of that magnitude is quickly untenable and astronauts would continuously accelerate.

If the force is perpendicular to the velocity, it is called centripetal acceleration. This acceleration is toward a center of rotation whereby velocity remains tangent to it, turning around a circumference. An initial energy input is required to trigger the rotation, but once it's started it conserves its angular momentum and kinetic energy without any further energy expense. The force arises from the tension that holds the structure intact as it rotates around its center of mass and this rotating structure can remain in any desired orbit – whether near the Earth, or around the Sun, Mars, or other planets.

Spin → Rotation, with its inherent centripetal acceleration, is the only viable means of providing artificial gravity. But this is not gravity as we know it on Earth. Cued by centripetal acceleration, astronauts perceive the center of rotation as "up." The strength of the apparent gravity is proportional to their distance from the center, and changes as they move up or down between decks at different radii. Moreover, their motions within the rotating habitat entail unwanted Coriolis accelerations and cross-coupled rotations that distort the apparent gravity. When moving vertically, one encounters a horizontal Coriolis force that pushes in an east/west direction (with or against the rotation tangent). When moving east/west, one experiences a vertical Coriolis force that induces the sensation of feeling heavier or lighter. Only motion north or south (parallel to the axis of rotation) is free from Coriolis effects.

Flow of fountain in artificial gravity (with angular velocity)
Sketch by Tye-Yan "George" Yeh

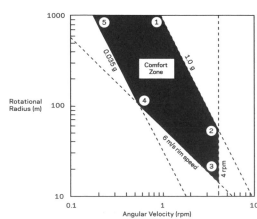

Comfort Zone graph

The turning of one's heads about any axis not aligned with the structure's rotation, induces gyroscopic effects in the body's vestibular organs that cause an illusory rotation around a mutually perpendicular axis. All of these undesirable side-effects can be minimized with a large radius of rotation but would maximize the structural mass and kinetic energy. Economics pushes in the opposite direction, toward a minimum tolerable radius, mass, and kinetic energy, which all exacerbate the gravitational distortion.

The vestibular organs in the inner ear have evolved to keep us oriented in terrestrial gravity. Even in the dark, when there is a lack of visual cues, they ensure balance. In micro gravity (weightlessness), the vestibular organs cease to function reliably because every transient change in motion causes a mismatched sense of orientation that contradicts visual sensations. This disaccord is a major cause of motion sickness. Astronauts often learn to disregard these vestibular signals and begin to rely more on vision to help maintain their sense of orientation. After returning to Earth, one Skylab astronaut in the familiar environment of his own home, fell down when the lights went out unexpectedly. The vestibular organs in artificial gravity encounter something that is not terrestrial nor micro gravity. Rather than reacting to random transient motions or simply shutting down, they respond to Coriolis accelerations and cross-coupled rotations at right angles to an astronaut's relative motion within his rotating habitat. The contrast with terrestrial gravity is greatest when the rotational radius is small and the spin rate is fast.

How is a space rendered inhabitable and meaningful? → To be meaningful, architecture must respond to the ambient environment with sensitivity and deliberation, with forms and systems that are comprehensible and relevant to the inhabitant's life. Designers realized that micro gravity would blur the concepts of floor, wall, and ceiling. Without weight to make things fall, any surface could be regarded in any of the three roles: the choice was arbitrary and essentially meaningless. As a practical matter, Raymond Loewy designed the Skylab wardroom with one particular surface designated as the "floor." Among other things, this helped to organize interior furnishings and partitions and facilitated ground-based training and familiarization with a backup module. In space, astronaut Ed Gibson reported that rotating more than 45 degrees away from the vertical orientation would render the wardroom unfamiliar. Skylab's larger workshop volume ("above" the wardroom) lacked any particular internal vertical orientation and as a result, was more disorienting. In response to the

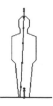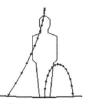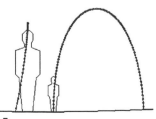

0-1
Earth intensity
centripetal
acceleration (1 g)

2
High angular
velocity (4 rpm)

3
High angular
velocity (4 rpm)

4
Low tangential
velocity (6 m/s)

5
Low centripetal acceleration (0.035 g) with
large radius (1000 m)

Skylab experience, space habitat designers now aim to provide a consistent vertical orientation, even though the choice of "vertical" is arbitrary in micro gravity. Micro gravitational space may be isotropic, but the human body is not.

Theory → In artificial gravity, due to Coriolis effects, not only are there three principal directions, but a minimum of five: up (toward the center of rotation), down (away from the center), east (tangential with the rotation), west (tangential against the rotation), and axial (parallel to the axis of rotation). Perhaps it follows that "eastwall" and "westwall" should be introduced as distinct concepts in architectural grammar. Unlike centripetal acceleration, which provides a constant sense of vertical, Coriolis acceleration and cross-coupled rotations are transient, proportionly related to

Interior for parabolic plane
umbilical design

In January 2004, the XERO company awarded umbilical design the contract to design the interior of a parabolic flight plane. Based in Kiruna, Sweden the XERO Corporation is set to offer zero-gravity flights to the public beginning in autumn 2005. The "XERO Experience invites individuals to 'defy gravity' and discover the unexpected, where normal things do not behave in normal ways." Lasting approximately 90 minutes, the planes will fly special parabolic flight profiles. During each parabola, passengers will experience 30 seconds of weightlessness – about the length of an average skydive. Throughout the XERO experience passengers will have the chance to defy gravity about 12-15 times by repeating this manoeuvre. XERO will provide this weightless experience aboard the IL76-MDK, a parabolic plane developed by the Russian space program. Originally designed for military puproses, the IL76-MDK lacks a consumer/comfort oriented interior. Because XERO leases the parabolic planes for several days at a time, umbilical's interior concept is designed to be extremely flexible and is based on a temporary, 14m long inflatable module that can be quickly installed and dismantled. Umbilical is also developing a mood lighting system where different tones and hues of lights help establish atmospheric sensations and also signal fluxuations in gravity changes. The incorporation of sound and fragrance will further enhance the interior space, generating a more reassuring envrionment. A primary goal of umbilical design is to incorporate space technologies into real world architecture, where development of mars/moon modules can be translated and applied to current architectural situations.

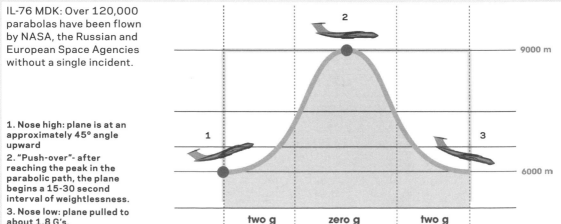

IL-76 MDK: Over 120,000 parabolas have been flown by NASA, the Russian and European Space Agencies without a single incident.

1. Nose high: plane is at an approximately 45° angle upward
2. "Push-over"- after reaching the peak in the parabolic path, the plane begins a 15-30 second interval of weightlessness.
3. Nose low: plane pulled to about 1.8 G's.

two g   zero g   two g

9000 m

6000 m

an inhabitant's motion. These transients might catch inhabitants off guard as they sit down, stand up, walk, tilt their heads, and go through myriad ordinary actions. Anything that helps the inhabitants maintain their sense of orientation, with respect to the rotation, would allow them to prepare for the consequences of their actions, aiding their coordination and adaptation to their rotating environment.

Space architecture is still in its infancy. Astronauts are carefully selected for their ability to adapt to difficult and unusual circumstances and architects have been hard pressed to refine space habitat design beyond what's needed for survival. Visual and vestibular systems are the most important mechanisms for human spatial orientation. In terrestrial gravity these typically reinforce each other but in micro gravity, the vestibular system ceases to provide useful input. It frequently conflicts with the visual system, signaling changes of orientation when no change can be seen. This conflict leads to motion sickness, until the brain learns to disregard the vestibular noise and visual signals begin to assume even more importance. In artificial gravity, the vestibular sense will be useful for distinguishing up and down, but it will also distinguish east and west due to Coriolis effects. To keep the visual system in sync, it seems wise to provide visual cues that acknowledge the vestibular sense. Other sensory modes – such as auditory, olfactory, or tactile – are possible contributors but seem to be much less significant to spatial orientation. (It must be noted that visually impaired people do learn to rely more on other sensory inputs – especially auditory and tactile.) How specifically to incorporate these signals into habitat design is an open question that can be adequately explored only by building and living in a variety of space habitats.

The long anticipated commercial boom in civilian space flight may be just around the corner. If so, the increased numbers and varied motives of the space-faring population will raise awareness of architectural issues that could impinge on general architectural theory. In particular, by moving away from terrestrial gravity to experience other gravities, we might for the first time come to fully appreciate the role of gravity in architecture.

Selected References

American Institute of Aeronautics and Astronautics, *Design Engineering Technical Committee*, Aerospace Architecture Subcommittee (2005). Home page. http://www.spacearchitect.org/ . Web site with an extensive bibliography and links to published papers on the general subject of space architect.

Connors, Mary M.; Harrison, Albert A.; Akins, Faren R (1985). *Living Aloft: Human Requirements for Extended Spaceflight* (NASA SP-483). NASA Scientific and Technical Information Branch. http://www.hq.nasa.gov/office/pao/History/SP-483/cover.htm.

Hall, Theodore W. (2005). "Artificial Gravity." http://www.artificial-gravity.com. Web site with links to published papers and software.

Hesselgren, Sven (1969). *The Language of Architecture*. Studentlitteratur, Lund, Sweden.

Hesselgren, Sven (1975). *Man's Perception of Man-Made Environment: An Architectural Theory*. Studentlitteratur, Lund, Sweden.

Johnson, Richard D.; Holbrow, Charles (eds) (1977). *Space Settlements: A Design Study* (NASA SP-413). NASA Scientific and Technical Information Office. http://lifesci3.arc.nasa.gov/SpaceSettlement/75SummerStudy/s.s.doc.html

Norberg-Schulz, Christian (1980). *Genius Loci: Towards a Phenomenology of Architecture*. Rizzoli.

Oberg, James E.; Oberg, Alcestis R. (1986). *Pioneering Space: Living on the Next Frontier*. McGraw-Hill.

Prak, Niels Luning (1968). *The Language of Architecture: A Contribution to Architectural Theory*. Mouton, the Hague, the Netherlands.

Thiis-Evensen, Thomas (1987). *Archetypes in Architecture*. Norwegian University Press.

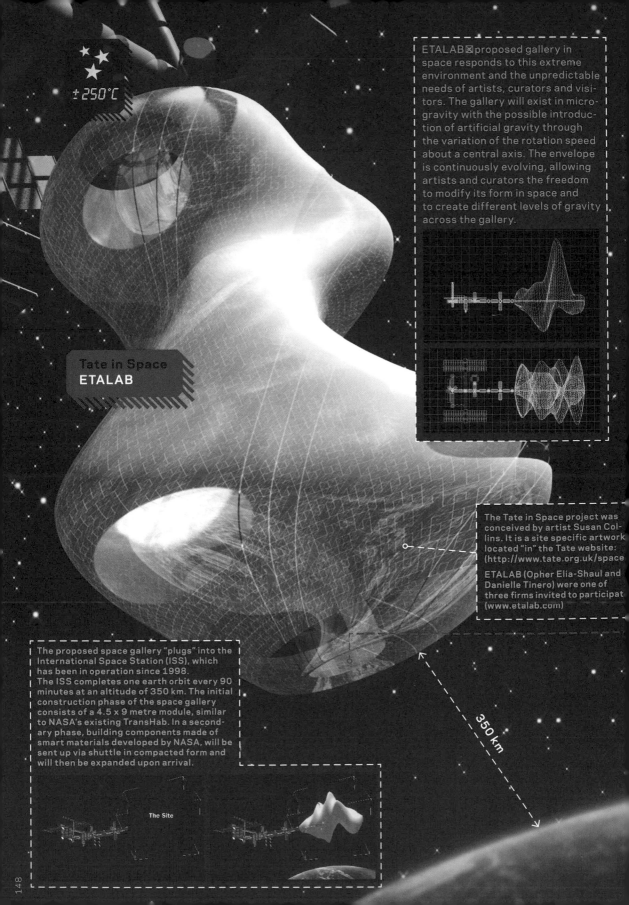

±250°C

Tate in Space
ETALAB

ETALAB⊠proposed gallery in space responds to this extreme environment and the unpredictable needs of artists, curators and visitors. The gallery will exist in microgravity with the possible introduction of artificial gravity through the variation of the rotation speed about a central axis. The envelope is continuously evolving, allowing artists and curators the freedom to modify its form in space and to create different levels of gravity across the gallery.

The Tate in Space project was conceived by artist Susan Collins. It is a site specific artwork located "in" the Tate website: (http://www.tate.org.uk/space

ETALAB (Opher Elia-Shaul and Danielle Tinero) were one of three firms invited to participat (www.etalab.com)

The proposed space gallery "plugs" into the International Space Station (ISS), which has been in operation since 1998. The ISS completes one earth orbit every 90 minutes at an altitude of 350 km. The initial construction phase of the space gallery consists of a 4.5 x 9 metre module, similar to NASA's existing TransHab. In a secondary phase, building components made of smart materials developed by NASA, will be sent up via shuttle in compacted form and will then be expanded upon arrival.

350 km

The Site

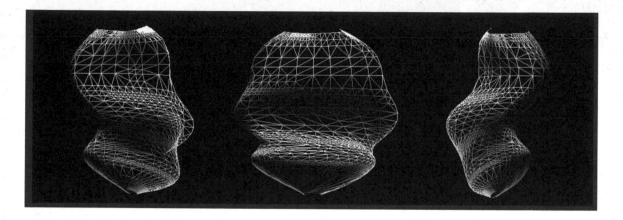

In a zero-gravity environment, ETALAB argues that earthly concepts such as floor, wall and ceiling cease to be distinct elements and may instead merge into one continuous, ever-changing surface. Liberated from certain conventional restrictions such as stairs or lifts, visitors in their proposed gallery would gain the freedom to move in all directions. This freedom creates a dynamic new physical and temporal relationship where people, artworks and architecture interact in zones of zero and partial gravity.

Intent on exploring technological and conceptual boundaries in architecture, ETALAB investigates the use of advanced technology materials to further enhance the flexibility of the gallery's external envelope. They suggest that "nextel," which is a visco-elastic cellular material capable of absorbing impact from meteorites and flying space debris, can be sandwiched between layers of woven Kevlar and Kapton sheets to produce a 30cm thick, layered material that is strong, lightweight and able to withstand extreme temperature fluxuations between +250° to -250° celcius. Additional advanced technology materials were proposed for the gallery's external skin to allow its reactive characteristics to be fully realized. These new materials would take their cue from nanotechonology and exploit human-like characteristics, operating in a similar way to muscles, cells and the nervous system. This flexibility would also enable the curator/artist to control levels of opacity, translucency and transparency of areas across the entire gallery.

Windows, seamlessly integrated into the skin would expand and contract like the lens of an eye to present magnified views of the earth and surrounding stars and space.

At the Architectural Body
Research Foundation, New York

verb

Shusaku Arakawa and Madeline Gins are artists, architects, poets and "co-ordinologists" – creative thinkers who integrate art, philosophy and science and put them into practice. They attempt to create new environments for the human body to activate the senses and rethink the very physical conditions of life and death. In extreme and simple fashion, Arakawa + Gins describe each of their projects as "a tool for learning how not to die": an attempt to reverse human destiny through space that serves the body to an extreme degree. After developing their work through installations, philosophical manifestos, plans and models, they have recently begun to construct some of these devices for change in the form of architecture.

A fictional housing project by Arakawa + Gins, in the form of a dialogue between the architects / coodinologists and visitors to the space. Beyond any traditional methods of creating architecture, the conversation describes an encompassing atmosphere of shifting spaces, forms and uses. An immersive, interactive apparatus that forces its users to react bodily, the first step towards a new environment for investigating nothing less than "what goes into being a person."

Architecture as Hypothesis
Arakawa + Madeline Gins

From Arakawa + Madeline Gins, *Architectural Body* (Tuscaloosa: University of Alabama Press, 2002).

Here is what architecture means to us: *a tentative constructing toward a holding in place.* Walk into this building and you walk into a purposeful guess. The built world floats a hypothesis or two as to how and by what the apportioned out comes to be everywhere, the everywhere.

ARAKAWA Here is the house we were telling you about.

ANGELA I don't see any house here.

GINS Granted this is not what in our time most people dream of coming home to.

ROBERT This heap?

GINS Yes, a low pile of materials that covers a fairly vast area.

ANGELA Are we at a dump? This low pile covering a vast area.

GINS What you take to be a pile of junk ranges in height from three to eleven inches. It measures close to 2,400 square feet – or 2,900 square feet if you include the courtyard.

ROBERT Courtyard?

GINS The shining part in the middle that has a lot of green around it.

ANGELA That's hilarious. Your house is shorter than its shrubbery.

ARAKAWA (laughs) I myself find that surprising. Shall we take a walk around it?

ROBERT Go around it? Why bother? I can see everything I need to from here.

GINS Isn't it wonderful that you can see all of it at once – as if you were looking at it in plan?

ANGELA That would make this pile of junk a very bumpy blueprint.

GINS Let's take ourselves around to the other side.

ROBERT Sure.

GINS Having made our way around the house, we are now on its south side.

ROBERT How about that! A huge stack of clothes has been thrown together. Assembled randomly? But the way it's piled up here on this side seems to be identical to how it has been stacked up over there at the northern end of the heap. Heights and depths differ, though.

ANGELA We were simply unable to discern the symmetry from the other side. It was only once we had moved around it that... Our being able to make out so much more from this vantage point, do we chalk that up to how the light is hitting it on this side, to what a northern light brings to the fore?

ROBERT Could it be that the intricate way things are piled on the left side – the west, I guess – closely resembles the pile or piles giving it its shape on the right – the east? I am actually beginning to spot some defined edges here and there.

GINS In which case I say we go in now. Do you want to go back around to the north side, or shall we enter from here?

ROBERT Diagonally opposite us... Is that an ordinary house over here?

ARAKAWA That's a tract house from the fifties.

ROBERT Where we are standing strikes me as somehow an extension of that house's front yard.

GINS Why don't we go back around this house to enter it through its front door.

ANGELA This – this whatever it is – has a front and a back?

GINS Of course.

ROBERT A front door by which to enter this doormat sort of thing, this giant shower cap...

GINS Here we are. Try to get in from, let me see, about here. You need to come back a few inches.

ANGELA How do you expect me to get into something this totally flat to the ground?

GINS You have to go under it. Pick it up and insert yourself into it.

ROBERT I can't get a hold of it. There's nothing to hold onto.

ANGELA Wow, it's so light! What material is this?

GINS A new material developed by NASA.

ANGELA Is it fireproof?

ARAKAWA Definitely, and waterproof. It's flexible, durable, and, to our delight, it happens to provide great insulation as well.

ANGELA That's unbelievable.

GINS Take that section of material you are holding in your left hand and push it up a little higher. Bring it up to at least waist level.

ANGELA Oh, here's something that looks like a handle. If I hold onto it to slide the material...

ARAKAWA You need to slide it to the left at the same time you push it upwards.

ANGELA Yes, it opened. This is scary. It keeps changing... volumes open with my every motion... With each push... it's changing right in front of my eyes, with each push... pushing open... opening. How I spread my arms to push it open... It takes shapes from how... If I push it to one side... It is as if I am that snail... How does that song go again?

GINS I have no trouble recalling that song whose lyrics are the parent text to this house's theme song. It goes like this:

Snails

But getting out of tight ground is quite another matter.
The more credit to them for going in,
given how much harder it is to get out.
Loving clumped earth, snails *go* along glued bodily to it.
They carry it with them, they eat it, they excrete it.
They *go* through it. It *goes* through them.

An interpenetration in the best possible taste
because, as it were, of complementary tones:
passive and active elements. The one simultaneously bathes and feeds the other,
which covers ground at the same time that it eats.
The moment it displays its nudity,
reveals its vulnerable form,
its modesty compels it to move on.
No sooner does it expose itself than it's on the go.

Note too that you cannot conceive of a snail
emerging from its shell and not moving.
The moment it stops to rest
it pulls back into its shell.

(Other things might be mentioned about snails. To begin with, their characteristic humidity. Their *sang froid*. Their extensibility.)

Snails *go* along glued bodily to first and second shells.
Clumped earth: second shell.
They carry it with them, they eat it, they excrete it.
They *go* through it. It *goes* through them.*

ROBERT That's heartening. I begin to see what is expected of us in here. First off, we need to stretch our limbs as much as possible. When I stretch my arms up as if I am about to hit a volleyball, the material rides up and... I can see a fairly large area. Is that a kitchen facility... a kitchen in the center?

GINS Yes, that is the kitchen. Your arms are raised up high. Atlas supporting the globe. And do you see where that gets you, it gets you a house that begins to have rooms.

---

*Both the theme song and its parent text use in full Francis Ponge's poem "Escargots." Ponge's snail musings adumbrate our concept of an architectural body. Did the poet go toward the snail, we wonder, with a similar concept in hand? Or – and this is more likely, given Ponge's express wish to be at all costs fair minded, that is, to take the side of things and creatures – did the gastropods simply present this to him, to a mammalian explorer, as a reward for his reportorial efforts on their behalf. In any case, there can be no doubt that, as great and as intimate as the human architectural heritage is, the architectural heritage of snails is as great and far more intimate. That the architectural know-how of this gastropod prefigures the concept of an architectural body, a concept that, for us, has been decades in the making, has as stark a reality for us as – now, little snail, cover your ears for a moment – the stabbing of an undersized fork into the body of an escargot, the plunking of it into one's mouth, and a biting into and a toothing through a muscularity god-awfully reminiscent of tongue. Francis Ponge, "Escargots," *Selected Poems*, translated by Margaret Gutton, John Montague, and C. K. Williams, edited by Margaret Gutton (Winston-Salem, N.C.: Wake Forest University Press, 1997), 38.

ANGELA Rooms form depending on how we move. If I bend down, I nearly lose the room. Would you open up the room a little more where you are?

ROBERT I will play a caryatid and you go off to the farthest end. I am beginning to feel more at ease within this. I find it much less strange. But, the thing is, the three of you now appear to me as a bit on the strange side. Are you emitting snail pheromones or something?

GINS You're at least four inches taller than the rest of us... so you probably should be the one to hold up the structure near the small hill by the window.

ROBERT Wow! It really opens up into a large area, despite its having an incredibly low ceiling. Lights come on as areas open.

ANGELA The floor is uneven. Does it slope?

GINS For a closer look at our effect on this house, let us each take a deep breath. The material expands and contracts as we do.

ROBERT Where do people sleep? Or take showers? What about cooking?

Everything that can be done in an ordinary house can be done in this one, but some maneuvering may be necessary to reach the point of sitting pretty. Each piece of material on the pile has ribs or spokes that open like those of an umbrella. Ready-to-be-activated expanding mechanisms lie at four-foot intervals. Depending on which setting has been selected, the house lies low, just as it was when you first saw it, and as it has remained all the while you've been in here, or it expands a little, getting some height, or, on the highest setting, it really achieves its full stature, including a dome and a vaulted ceiling. There's a setting to accommodate anything you want to do in the house. For example, you had asked before about how feasible it was to light a stove and do some cooking. Cooking can take place within an ample kitchen that forms and stays formed until one selects a lower setting that causes the material to close back in and down. We predict that drawing the unfurled material back and down to be within touching distance will be a high priority for most inhabitants of houses like this. Remote control switches operate sensors that bloom and fabricate the house on behalf of those who are ill or handicapped. You are not given a finished house but instead form it through your movements and through those of whoever else is in there with you. All materials are impervious to weather.

For people have entered a work of architecture that floats the Sited Awareness Hypothesis or, as it is also known, the Architectural Body Hypothesis. Upon being entered and used, this work of architecture, which only becomes what it is through being entered and used, gives corroborating evidence for this hypothesis. Architecture as hypothesis plays off of the long-short story of architecture as non-hypothesis. Constructed to exist in the tense of *what if*, it presents itself as intentionally provisional, replacing definite form with tentative form, the notion of a lasting structure with that of an adaptive one.

GINS Yes, cooking – that doesn't present a problem. The house has a full complement of rooms. Whatever people do in ordinary houses, they can do in this.

ROBERT You mean people can actually live here?

GINS Of course. I was hoping you'd want to.

ARAKAWA Live here and do daily research.

ROBERT Research into what?

ARAKAWA Into what goes into being a person. This place can help you do that. What part of the house do you think you're in now?

ANGELA I haven't the foggiest idea. But I at least have it in me now to feel it to be one room or another. I'm interested in doing that research you speak of.

GINS We've entered the living room. We probably should sit down and rest for a while, so let's head for the couch and chairs.

ROBERT Oh, really?

GINS Since the living room remains missing, we will have to stretch out and reach up to form it. Have you ever pitched a tent?

ROBERT Not one this large. I have some nice memories of watching a crew put up a huge tent for a friend's wedding... and then of being inside it.

GINS Let's see. There are four of us, so that means we have four poles available. Of course, on a higher setting the structure could rally many more poles... as many as needed.

ROBERT But if I am going to be a tent pole or caryatid, how can I also sit in a chair?

ARAKAWA If we initiate the form, other spines within the surrounding material will kick in and take over... for ten minutes at a time.

GINS Of course, it would really get going and open up if we had the house on one of its higher settings, one that engages the whole set of spine-deploying mechanisms embedded in the fabric.

ANGELA How many settings does this living space have?

GINS Three. A zero setting that we call the *snail setting*. And then a medium setting, in which the material stays always at a slight remove from those within it; we have named this the *close-to-snail setting*. The highest setting is the one that does it all; when this is on, spine-deploying mechanisms are fully engaged; we have named it *roomy*.

ROBERT At this moment... you have it on the snail setting, I think it would be fair to say. All the while... always turned to that?

ARAKAWA Snail setting all along. This setting pro- vides the most intense way to use this... tool... this piece of equipment. This house is a tool, a procedural one.

GINS A functional tool, whether it be a hammer, a telephone, or a telescope, extends the senses, but a procedural tool examines and reorders the sensorium.

ARAKAWA Let us then cloak ourselves in solemnly merry stanzas that guide us in the use of this piece of equipment within which we are moving.

Humansnails

But getting out of tight spots is quite another matter.
The more credit to them for picking up an edge and going in,
given how much harder it is to get out.
Loving *their* medium, humansnails *go* along glued bodily to it,

all their breathing closing in palpably around them.
They carry this with them, they swallow it,
they expel, exude, and disperse it.
They *go* through it. It *goes* through them.

Their medium: sited awareness
All that a humansnail disperses: (its) ubiquitous site.
Call all that a humansnail disperses: (its) architectural body.
An interpretation in the best possible taste because, as it were, of complementary tones: passive and active elements. The one simultaneously bathes and feeds the other,
which covers the distance it breathes in and out and forms.

Humansnails go along glued bodily to second skins or shells (architectural surrounds).
First shells: shaped volumes of the beloved medium of humansnails.
First shells: shaped volumes that form by virtue of actions humansnails take within second shells (architectural surrounds).
First shells: relatively large atmospheric globular samples of the beloved medium – medium as oneself?? – that wraps around humansnails.
First shell: on-the-spot humansnail-made wrappings of sited awareness.
Have the man-made become as to the point as the snail-made.

Thick with one's own breathing.
thick with one's own landing-site configurations.
They carry landing sites with them, they swallow them,
heuristically for a direct mapping.
They expel, exude, and disperse landing-site configurations.
They *go* through their ubiquitous sites,
i.e., the sum of all landing sites of each moment.
Their ubiquitous site *go* through them.

Note too that you cannot conceive of a humansnail emerging from its shells and not moving.
The moment it stops to rest it pulls back into its next pair of shells.

(Other things might be mentioned about humansnails. To begin with, their characteristic timidity. Their *sang froid*. Their extensibility.)

A person's landing-site dispersal usually does not straightforwardly present itself as "breathing material." How dare we put scare quotes around the breathable massenergy of the universe turned world?! Oh to have the opportunities of a snail!! Would that you could check up on what disperses under your auspices as what you feel yourself to be. Your actions cling to you and respond to you as if they were growing out of you like fingernails. Your house becomes your pet or you become the pet of your house, or a mixture of the two.

ANGELA It's time for us to move through it now, isn't it?

ARAKAWA It sure is. I'm bringing my hands down to my sides and bending slightly forward and just plunging ahead. Each of you should assume a similar posture and then forge ahead. Each goes off in a different direction.

ROBERT When do we get out of the snail phase?

GINS Well, you know, it's possible to dwell in this house for days on end without ever moving it off the snail setting. I think for this, your first time in it, we should probably leave the dial where it is. It's the most direct way we know to reorder sensateness... sensitivity... sensibility... one's sensorium... landing-site dispersal... site awareness.

ANGELA As a way to engineer that direct mapping the two of you speak of? If so, what should we do? Should we move around more?

ARAKAWA With less to attend to in this snail-setting living room than in ordinary ones, it becomes easier to focus in on the effect each action has. Come toward me, toward this couch, moving in an exaggeratedly slow way. Can you see it from where you are?

ROBERT I see no couch. I can't even see you at this point.

ARAKAWA Then move toward the sound of my voice. Go a little slower.

ROBERT I have spotted a couch leg.

GINS Head toward it – still in slow motion – and, as you do, describe everything you see and feel.

ROBERT Something that extends from the back of my head all the way down along the broad of my back to a little below my waist pushes me forward. And with every step, I feel and see a bobbing horizon, a low one, a horizon that I look down to actually. As I carefully dole out the movements that constitute this step I am taking, using tiny haulings-up and miniscule pushings-through to lift my right leg, I see being added to a room – a room? – that moments before had within it only a single couch leg, what I make out to be your foot, and Angela's frame from her shoulders on down. Angela, I cannot believe how much you are swaying.

ARAKAWA That little group you describe equals your ubiquitous site, everywhere you have landed or could land. Call all that which is in the immediate vicinity of a person a ubiquitous site.

GINS This is a ubiquity of *you*... inclusive of... your power to compose a world and be in contact with it... inclusive of all contact, of whatever variety, you have with the world.

ARAKAWA Defined to let loose an everywhere at once, the word *ubiquitous* even so fails to convey this covering of everywhere at once we experience in here. The rapid succession of events called experience overreaches ubiquity, I guess.

GINS The number of purposeful actions required of you has been suddenly greatly reduced. It becomes easier to observe yourself as an agent of action because this closed-in world exacts fewer purposive moves.

ARAKAWA Even so, there is still a semblance of an agent and there is still a great scattering.

GINS Yes, it becomes predominantly a world of landing sites. Down to that level of abstraction.

ARAKAWA Each of us becomes an everywhere evenly distributed agent, dropping the centralizing habit that members of our species have had for such a terribly long time. What I am about to say might sound irrational to you – but if it turns out to be what is going on, then rationality will have to be redefined. An everywhere evenly distributed agent – a ubiquitous site or an architectural body – will even be able to re-negotiate gravity.

GINS The gravity that gets accorded to apportioning out, for a more complete picture, probably ought to be spoken of as an apportioning out and in.

ROBERT It feels as if the material will go from only clinging to my back to fully engulfing me. With each thrusting of my limbs, or head and neck, or torso against the house that sits on top of me and drapes over me, I find myself in drastically changed circumstances.

ARAKAWA When in the snail setting, the house only has rooms that the actions taken within it produce.

GINS You are casting about as you always do, but with a difference. In the snail setting, the feel of the house and its weight cast you even before you can start casting about on your own. Through its casting of you, through its determining of how you came to be kinesthetically and proprioceptively disposed, the house prompts your actions. How we have been cast, how we are kinesthetically disposed, determines how we choose to act and if we can.

ARAKAWA Closing in on you, the tactile surroundings sculpt kinesthetic possibility or kinesthetic with-it-ness. This sculpted kinesthetic with-it-ness – the tentativeness of any moment – can be thought of as the matrix of person.

GINS Kinesthesia – body feel or bodily feeling – can never be had apart from imagining. To begin with, to move at all... One needs to image, for example, where to place one's arm prior to moving it.

ANGELA Everything is responsive to my every move. I am at the wide-open part of an enclosure shaped like a side pocket of a pair of slacks. The draping material extends out from my neck and shoulders down toward the pocket's narrow end. This end is not sewn in place but is instead a temporary horizon, bobbing, all activated by... my every move.

ROBERT Being within this enclosure makes landing more palpable.

ANGELA As far as landing goes: the material lands on me, upon me. Through its actions, my body "lands punches" on the material. The activated bobbing-up-and-down horizon that is draped into shifting place lands ever differently. A lot depends on whether I land on my feet or not.

GINS I must say that what we have enclosed in here, within, as you aptly describe it, a shallow pocket, is "that which registers."

ARAKAWA The body has a spherical kinesthetic-proprioceptive-tactile dispersive potential, tentativeness at the ready.

GINS There is that which can register whatever turns up... The registering are the landing sites we speak of.

ARAKAWA We would like to be able to keep track of all that gets registered at any given moment. That within this pocket one has far fewer than the usual number of things and events to take note of suits our purpose well.

ROBERT Fewer things to keep track of in the outside world, but as far as the body is concerned nothing changes: the number of places in the body that need at each moment to be kept track of stays roughly the same, doesn't it?

ARAKAWA Yes and no. The number of landing sites particular to the body itself stays within a predictable range, which happens to be a fairly wide one. But with the house on the snail setting, the number of strictly bodily landing sites cluster at the high end of that range.

GINS In addition to standing stock still, close your eyes for a moment. What do you find as your body?

ROBERT I find my body to be at the mercy of this material that doesn't leave it alone. Always lightly resting on my back and responsive to my every move, this thing you call a house threatens to...

GINS At how many spots along your back would you say you feel it? You know, any registering of a point of physical contact equals a tactile landing site.

ARAKAWA If the contact feels continuous, then you have probably joined several smaller tactile landing sites into a few large ones. Your head, neck, shoulders, back: a single landing site or two.

GINS It might be a good idea to try to re-divide them, that is, to approximate how they might have been before they were combined. Tactile landing sites report: that is there. Coupled with kinesthetic landing sites and imaging landing sites they report: that is there as that.

ROBERT It is as if I had been turned into a statue of myself... not the caryatid of before. From the points of contact – tactile landing sites, I guess – forward I am entering into, or feeling into, the feel of my tissues. Ubiquitous tissues feel to me to be very breath-like but simultaneously not that breath-like.

GINS Kinesthetic landing sites are of course closely allied with tactile landing ones. Often tactile landing sites will prompt kinesthetic ones to come alive. Because you are being so tactilely activated from behind, your kinesthetic-pro-prioceptive wherewithal is now being cast with a decidedly frontal orientation. Tactility and kinesthesia toggle-switch into one another, so, were you to suddenly happen to bring your hand to your chest, kinesthesia would immediately give way to tactility at that spot.

ROBERT About kinesthesia... I feel all porous and it, kinesthesia, functions as that which animates porosity. I am a filter, and this shallow pocket we are within is another, a different type of filter, perhaps a slightly more porous one. Rapid exchanges are going on between these two filters, and the speed and quality of the exchange depends on how my body... My body casts about within this material and then actions and events cast my body. A lot depends on how that sculpture, my cast body of felt sense, goes on to cast the rest of the pocket's volume.

ARAKAWA Because your eyes have been closed, it would seem that what you have described has been imaged. But as all description springs into action within kinesthetic-proprioceptive bounds, your visualizing of your body with your eyes closed has surely been produced by perceptual as well as imaging landing sites. This ought not to come as a surprise to anyone; but nearly everyone finds this to be surprising. Open your eyes.

ROBERT Wow!! It's all so different. But I remained motionless, as you instructed me to, and so, I be- lieve, did the rest of you. It could not have been only our breathing that so greatly altered this place.

GINS And yet... to the extent that breathing is sufficient to change landing site configuration... As abstractions that act as conduits for apportioning out, landing sites... Or landing sites may be abstractions, but they are ones designed to let that which gets apportioned out, that which is prior to abstracting, flow through with the minimal amount of interference. What, I should ask you, is landing for you now?

ANGELA The entire house is landing on me... on us. There are so many landings I hardly know where to begin.

ROBERT When I breathe in there are a lot of landings as a result of that... I am feeling my breathing more than I ever have before. What I breathe in lands in the lung... but I can't exactly track it to there, although in a way I can. But my attending to all this breathing... my solicitousness to my own breathing, would you characterize all that taken together as landing?

ARAKAWA Yes, I think so. I am thrilled that you came up with that. Linking breathing and landing... we hadn't quite gotten to that yet.

ANGELA What a cozy spot. If you don't mind, I think I will curl up right here and take a nap.

verb The first built work of Arakawa + Gins outside of a museum envrionment is an enormous theme park in Yoro, titled Reversible Destiny. Unlike most theme parks, this one has no rides, no machines, no advertisements and no images. Next to it sits another "park": a small house that repeats the themes of the landscape as architecture.

Yoro Reversible Destiny,
Yoro city, Gifu prefecture, Japan

Architecture, in anyone's definition of it, exists primarily to be at the service of the body. The question arises as to how to be most fully at the service of the body. Who would not want to live in a world built to serve the body to the nth degree? (…)

Three decades ago, by wedding the word *reversible* with the term *destiny*, a supposedly set-in-stone sequence of events, we announced a war on mortality…. Architecture is the greatest tool available to our species, both for figuring itself out and for constructing itself differently.

From *Architectural Body*, by Arakawa and Madeline Gins (Tuscaloosa: The University of Alabama Press, 2002).

verb

10°C

The next stage of the Reversible Destiny project is a model house in Shidami, built by Nagoya City and the Nagoya City Housing Corporation to coincide with the opening of the 2005 World Exposition in Aichi. Built as a prototype that can aggregate to form a city, the house is designed for minimal energy consumption through the use of recycled materials and natural resources like solar and wind energy. During the Expo, the project welcomes visitors while housing a living experiment with actual inhabitants.

External Genome Park
Arakawa + Madeline Gins

From New York all the way to Shidami, Japan

Reversible Destiny Project Site → The basic plan of the project as it grows into a city. The total project will have a gently sloped topography with a community space at the center. Every house is surrounded by plants and vegetable gardens, with a complex shape that allows its users to discover the senses of the body.

Construction process idea

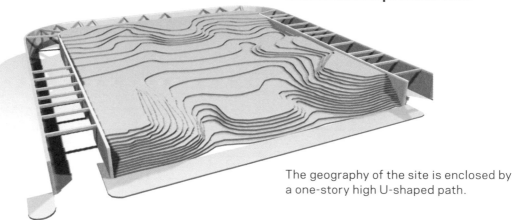

The geography of the site is enclosed by a one-story high U-shaped path.

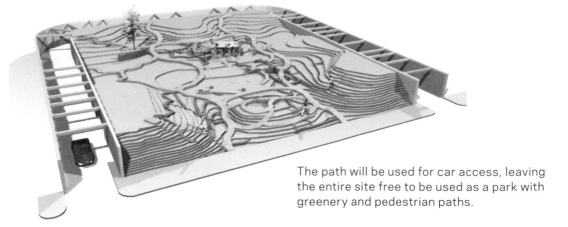

The path will be used for car access, leaving the entire site free to be used as a park with greenery and pedestrian paths.

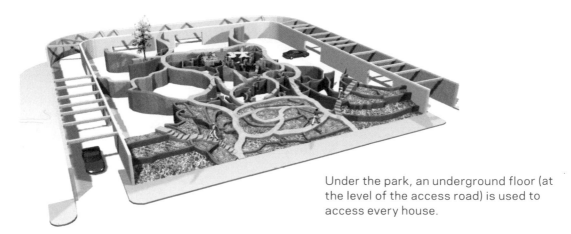

Under the park, an underground floor (at the level of the access road) is used to access every house.

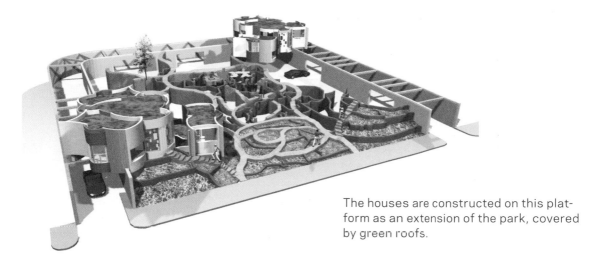

The houses are constructed on this platform as an extension of the park, covered by green roofs.

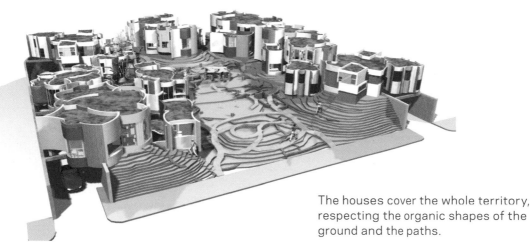

The houses cover the whole territory, respecting the organic shapes of the ground and the paths.

New houses are stacked to form a new geography covered with natural materials. The center remains open as a public space where visitors and neighbors can meet.

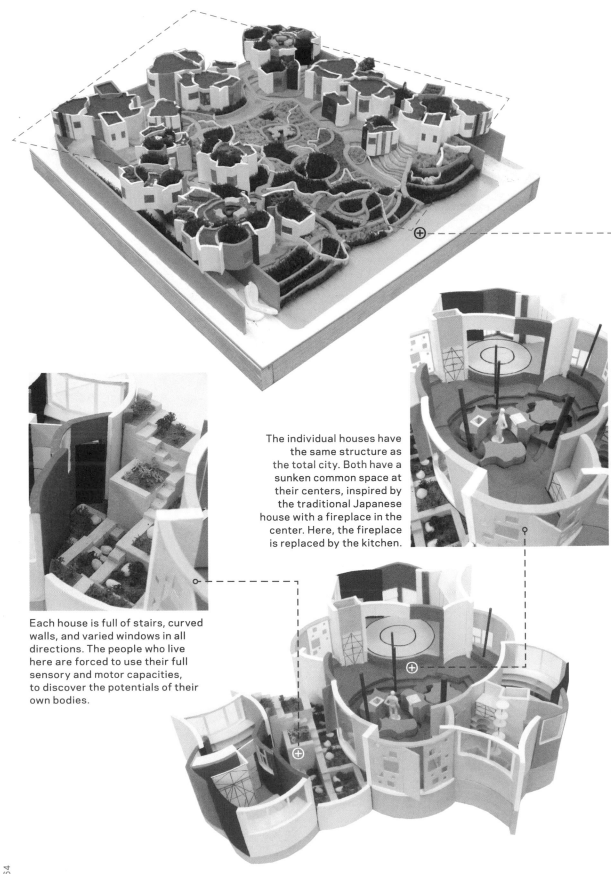

The individual houses have the same structure as the total city. Both have a sunken common space at their centers, inspired by the traditional Japanese house with a fireplace in the center. Here, the fireplace is replaced by the kitchen.

Each house is full of stairs, curved walls, and varied windows in all directions. The people who live here are forced to use their full sensory and motor capacities, to discover the potentials of their own bodies.

↖ A view from the round Tatami room back towards the center of the house.
↗ A view from the sunken kitchen. From here, It is possible to see every room, with lots of windows and three entrance doors.
↘ The house's innabitants understand the space, through more than just visual information, by touching and feeling like babies. 78 different plans were designed in collaboration with experimental psychologists and 300 other academics.

data **External Genome Park, Shidami →** Location: Aichi, Japan. **Design:** Arakawa + Madeline Gins (Architectural Body Research Foundation). **Client:** Nagoya City Housing Corporation. **Collaboration:** Toho Gas Co., Ltd., INAX Corporation, Hitachi Ltd., CHUBU Electric Power Co., Inc. **Cooperative collaboration:** The Japan Association for the 2005 World Exposition. **Construction period:** April 2004 - March 2005. **Plot area:** 2,000 m². **Building area:** 380.68 m². **Floor area:** 582.98 m². **Number of floors:** 2. **Number of houses:** 7. **Structure:** Reinforced concrete. **Photographs:** Sakae Fukuoka (© Nagoya City Art Museum). **www.reversibledestiny.org**

At the next construction site, Tokyo, April 2005

verb

9°C

The next Reversible Destiny project, a community of stacked housing blocks in Tokyo, is now under construction. The design of the units forces inhabitants to pay constant attention to their own movements and perceptions of space: sloped floors, curved walls, low ceilings, scattered and inclined windows... An architecture that demands attention, but one that provides an alternative form of barrier-free housing, fully inhabitable even by the elderly.

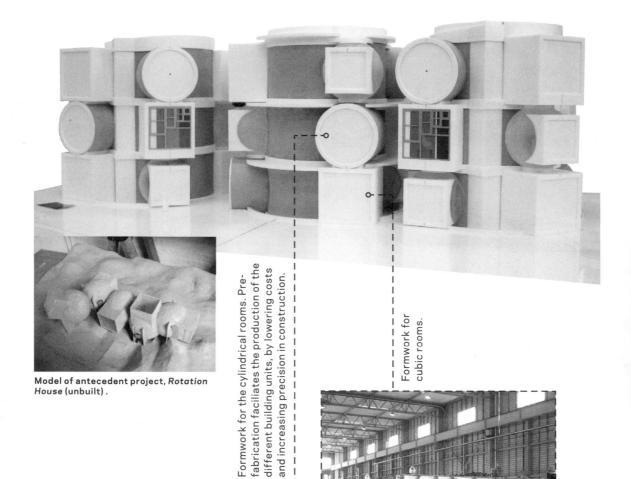

Model of antecedent project, *Rotation House* (unbuilt).

Formwork for the cylindrical rooms. Pre-fabrication faciliates the production of the different building units, by lowering costs and increasing precision in construction.

Formwork for cubic rooms.

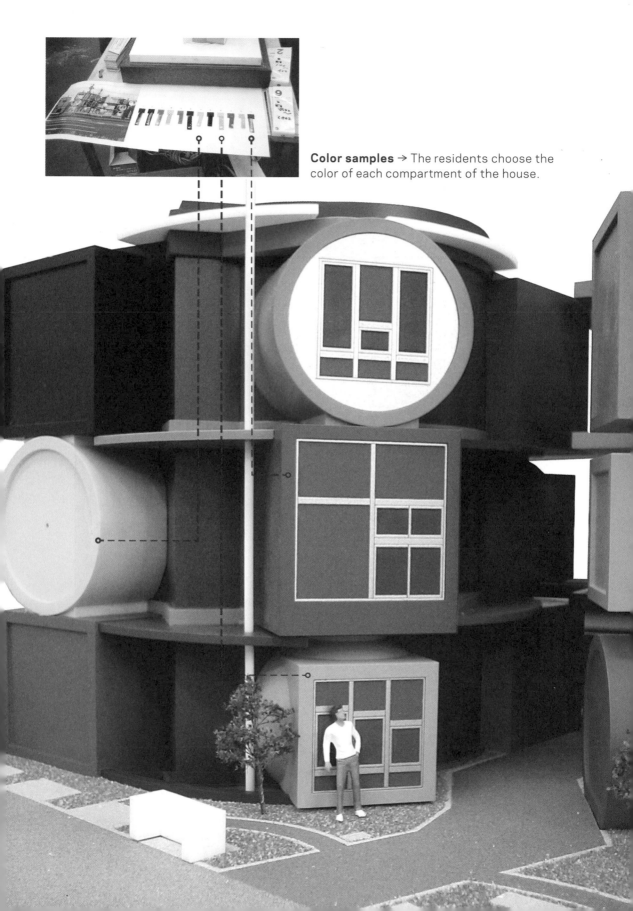

Color samples → The residents choose the color of each compartment of the house.

Individual rooms → Each apartment has two or three rooms and a bathroom, connected by a round common space housing the kitchen and dining areas. A circular ring of balconies extend between the cubic, cylindrical and spherical rooms.

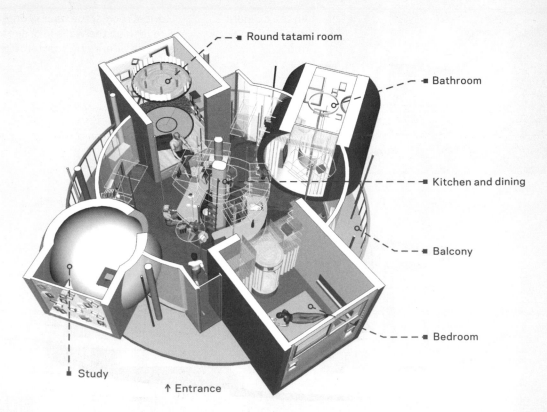

- Round tatami room
- Bathroom
- Kitchen and dining
- Balcony
- Bedroom
- Study
↑ Entrance

data

Reversible-Destiny Lofts Mitaka in Memory of Helen Keller → Location: Mitaka, Tokyo, Japan. **Design:** Arakawa + Madeline Gins (Architectural Body Research Foundation), Yasui Architects & Engineers, Inc. **Construction:** Takenaka Corporation. **Construction period:** October 2004 - ongoing. **Plot area:** 452.96 m². **Building area:** 260 m². **Floor area:** 760 m². **Number of floors:** 3. **Number of houses:** 9 (70m²/ house). **Structure:** Reinforced concrete. **Photographs:** ABRF, Inc. **www.reversibledestiny.org**

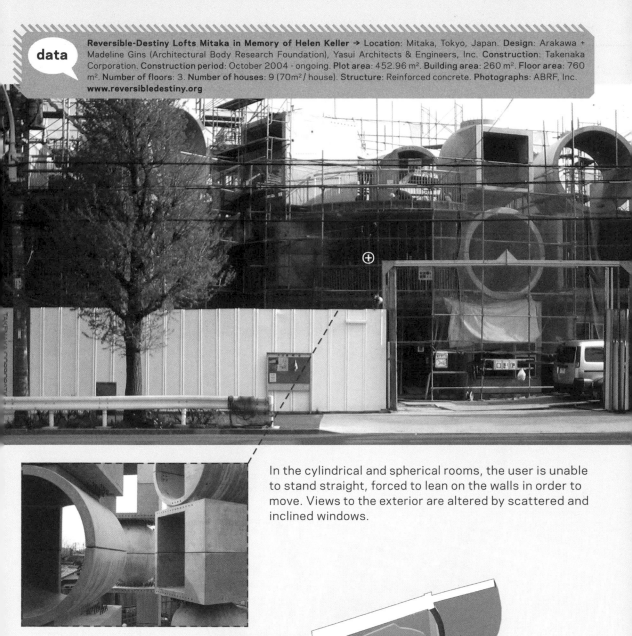

In the cylindrical and spherical rooms, the user is unable to stand straight, forced to lean on the walls in order to move. Views to the exterior are altered by scattered and inclined windows.

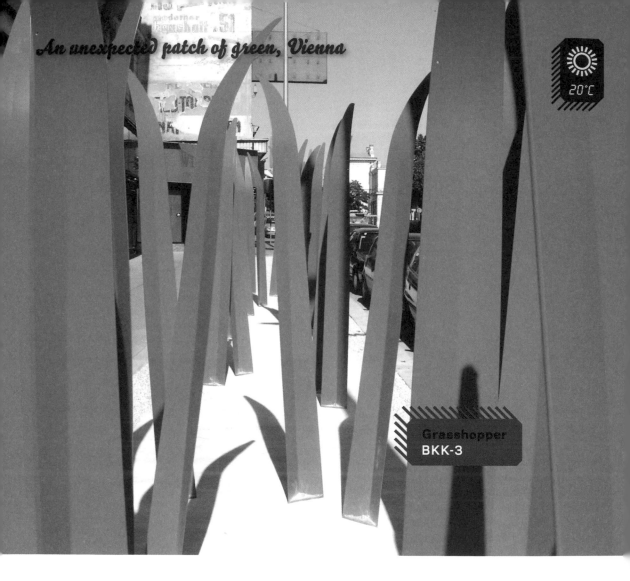

20°C

Grasshopper
BKK-3

When we planned the IP.TWO trade and office centre we had the strong feeling that the front of the
building needed something. IP.TWO is located in
Vienna – at the corner of a heavy-traffic thorough-
fare and music-entertainment/bar-mile.
The program requirements consisted of:
  1. A connection to the first floor restaurant
  2. A public space
  3. A multifunctional space for events
  4. An interesting design to be seen from the
      100,000 cars that pass by daily.
The only way to build what we suggested in
the design brief was to present the proposal
as an art project sponsored by the City's Art
Department. When we asked the city coun-
cil for support they loved the idea of a public
space sculpture. They told us it should reflect
the young character of the district, SOHO

Ottakring. We then decided to make a funny, fresh design. Because the Grasshopper was to be an art project used by everyone, it couldn't be a normal pedestrian bridge. It's our philosophy that art can be funny and useful and we believe that in order to work seriously nonsense must be given a chance. Our initial ideas were connected to freshness and we made some drafts with oversized vegetables, like broccoli. However, the production costs would have been too expensive so we changed the idea to grass. After that switch the design came together.

The Grasshopper is located at the Gürtel, which lies under the Otto Wagner railway and is one of the biggest urban renewal projects in Vienna. The project needed to work on both the individual and urban scale. It measures about 50 meters in length, which is large enough to make a strong urban intervention, but, small enough to be remain interesting and funny on the individual scale. Currently, many people hang out there at night or have celebrated their New Year's at the Grasshopper.

This autumn a passing driver suggested that we remove the plants before wintertime, otherwise they would die. A perfect illusion – it's incredible how good it is to see a "green" space in the wintertime, and more so in the snow.

The majority of the public reacted in a positive way. However, two 'blades of grass' have been destroyed by vandals. These last developments were at the behest of the surrounding districts because they also would like "grass" in their neighborhoods. (We are developing plans for installing a wider cultivation of these installations). We investigated many materials because we wanted to make the grass flexible and smooth. We dreamed of grass that would be touchable and could vibrate. However, many early proposals were too expensive or were not long-lasting or durable enough for long term use. Because this is a public area we had to prepare the space for people who might be aggressive or want to destroy the grass.

In the end, we chose to make the blades of grass out of massive steel covered with a special green coating.

We do not like the classic architectural photography where pictures are taken in an empty room. In most of our pictures you will see moving people because we prefer to see the proportions of a space. Vienna is the city of horses and the "Fiaker," so we took Lucy – a typical beautiful Viennese horse and placed her in our photos. ■

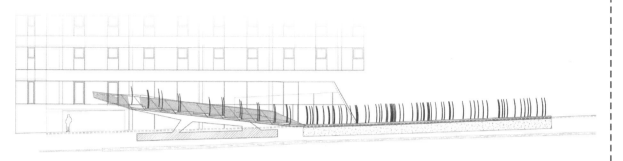

 data

Grasshopper, Vienna, Austria → Location: 1160 Wien, Lerchenfeldergürtel. Client: SIAG/Prisma. **Design:** BKK-3. Building contractor: Lang & Menhofer. Structure: Fröhlich & Locher, Wien. **Construction period:** August 2004. Plot area: 200 m². **Floor area:** 48 m². **Structure:** Steel, reinforced concrete. Dimensions: 22 x 3.20 m, maximum height 4.10 m. **Net building costs:** 70.000€. Photographs: BKK-3 and Hertha Hurnaus. **www.bkk-3.com**

An imaginary forest in the Heyri Art Valley, South Korea

Invented to market fashion products, Dalki is a cartoon character inhabiting a garden with her friends. Located in the Heyri Art Valley development, Dalki Theme Park is a building where these characters interact with visitors in a space for shopping, playing, eating, lounging and exhibits dealing with scale and nature. Learned dichotomies (imaginary/real, shopping/play, natural/synthetic, site/building, culture/commerce) and scale differences create a "disbelief" that impedes users from fully engaging the realization of this imaginary world. Borrowing literary strategies for the suspension of disbelief, the fluid organization of space and program blurs these dichotomies and eases users into the "story" of Dalki.

Dalki Theme Park "I like Dalki!"
Mass Studies, Slade Architecture, Ga.A Architects

Dalki theme park is a place where imaginary creatures interact with human visitors in a real setting. This proposition poses challenging questions:
How are the boundaries between the real and the imaginary world defined and negotiated?
At what point in this relation between the imagined and the real should the encounter between users and characters occur?
Is the definition of a point even possible?
How to maintain the aura of the imagined – the unreal – once it becomes physical?

Korea's Happy Towns / James Slade

Development in Korea is characterized by extreme opportunism. Modeled on the Japanese paradigm, it can also be seen as a reaction to the socialist regime of North Korea. Buildings and land are commodities, maximizing building area is often the main design criteria; land is not seen as a landscape but as a base upon which to place a building. Concurrent with this type of development and the hyper-opportunistic pursuit of profit have been the many voices lamenting the density and disorder of the urban environment in Seoul and throughout Korea.

In this context, new towns have been planned to offer a more harmonious model of living. Sometimes these are purely commercial ventures. Often they are organized around a religious theme and sponsored by powerful church groups. The most recent developments in Heyri Art Valley and Paju Book City look towards culture, and in particular the arts, as their unifying themes. These developments, adjacent to the Demilitarized Zone (DMZ) north of Seoul, are classified as reunification zones by the government's Sunshine Policy, which foresees economic and social cooperation with North Korea leading to an open relationship between the two countries.

Created to become a hub for artistic production and creative thought, Heyri is a planned community occupying vacant land that was formerly a military training ground in Gyeonggi province, northwest of Seoul. The master plan, by a group of well respected Korean architects headed by Jong-Kyu Kim and Jun-Sung Kim, foresees a 'rural city' of 370 buildings, each less than three stories tall, for writers, directors, artists and others involved in cultural/artistic production. The plan calls for a community developed around 'the principles of an environmentally friendly urban landscape', merging the mixed-use characteristics of a city with the open, low-rise development of a suburb. Each area contains both residential and cultural/community programs. There is also a network of paths and hardscape areas to encourage mixing and to foster a stronger sense of community.

The Heyri master plan strategy looked to the landscape to generate the form of the development, converting the structure of the land into the structure of the city – counter to the typical development in Seoul. In Heyri, the master plan was organized around the five "mountains" that existed on the site and were left as green "natural" areas, conforming the new development to the topography of these hills. The landscape is now a point of differentiation, an asset rather than a pure commodity. The very idea of natural is questioned with this act of willful preservation.

Unlike themed developments in the United States, such as Florida's Seaside, that tend to focus on leisure, getaways and a small town typology (the characteristics of New Urbanism), the theme in Korea is more often centered on production – whether cultural production in Heyri or literary production in Paju Book City, another nearby development. The master plan requires that a percentage of every building be dedicated to cultural or social/group activity. This organization is not a nostalgic return to the past, but a forward-looking, optimistic projection of an idealized future.

The Dalki Theme Park reads as a sixth "mountain" in the existing landscape. Rather than abstracting from nature, the building is a synthetic hyper-representation of nature (meta-real), mimicking while questioning the "nature" of nature. One of the mountains closest to the building has already been flattened for a new commercial shopping center, turning it into the virtual stunt double of this displaced mountain.

Above the forest → A roof garden with natural vegetation.

Inside the trees → An enclosed retail space with Dalki character products and a play area.

Under the forest → covered outdoor space between pilotis

The site of "I Like Dalki" belongs to the Korean fashion company Ssamzie, known for its innovative marketing strategies and its sponsorship of young Korean art, which includes the artist in residence program 'Ssamzie Space.' The client initially wanted us to design a storage and exhibition space for their collection, but after a few meetings we were presented with a radically different program: A 'theme park / flagship brand space' for their character business "I Like Dalki."

The warehouse-gallery was eventually added again to the brief during the construction design phase, and located adjacent to the theme park in the form of a thin slab building. The client brought a collection of visual materials, mostly conventional Disney-like imagery, as a guideline or starting point for our design. The main building was rendered like a European castle (which they called the 'fortress of giants'), with a series of structures that looked like forest huts for Hobbits dispersed in the surrounding open space (called

'forest of giants'). As an initial step, this suggested that "I Like Dalki" would have to be something different, something that had not existed before, suitable to the size of the plot and the attributes of the Heyri development.

Since the building was about negotiating the boundary between the imagined (cartoon characters) and the real (visitors), we found that the play of scales could be an effective strategy to maintain the aura of the imagined in the physical environment.

Another initial idea was to create a built/synthetic environment that worked like a forest and would seem part of the natural surroundings. The idea of a 'forest building' led us to organize the experiences into three different levels: under the forest, inside of the forest tree mass, and on top of the forest. The forest top became a roof garden with natural vegetation; inside the tree mass, an enclosed retail space with Dalki character products and a play area; under the forest, a covered outdoor space between pilotis. What could have been merely a commercial box was transformed into a structure that doubled the open space for public use, distributed on two levels with an interior retail level sandwiched between them.

The building presents a negotiable surface with no strict programmatic or physical boundaries, a changing topology that presents options for occupation. This strategy helps blur the boundaries between public space, shopping space, interior and exterior, natural and artificial, providing resistance to the shopping program – which itself resists public space/occupation. The model for this softly defined space is a child's outlook on the world, where the boundaries between things are much less clearly defined. The loose categorization of "play" became our organizational model. The building defines three vertical zones; scaleless artificial garden and sky at the ground level, flowing mixed program space on the main level, and a garden and lounge on the roof that extends the four surrounding hills of the lush natural landscape. Sculpted floor planes merge these levels into each other and into the site to create a seamless transition between zones: interior to exterior, building to landscape, and program to program. The vertical stacking allows short circuits: like hypertext in HTML, users can jump from one space/program to another. Together the smooth flowing spaces, mixed program distribution and short circuits allow users to choreograph their experiences.

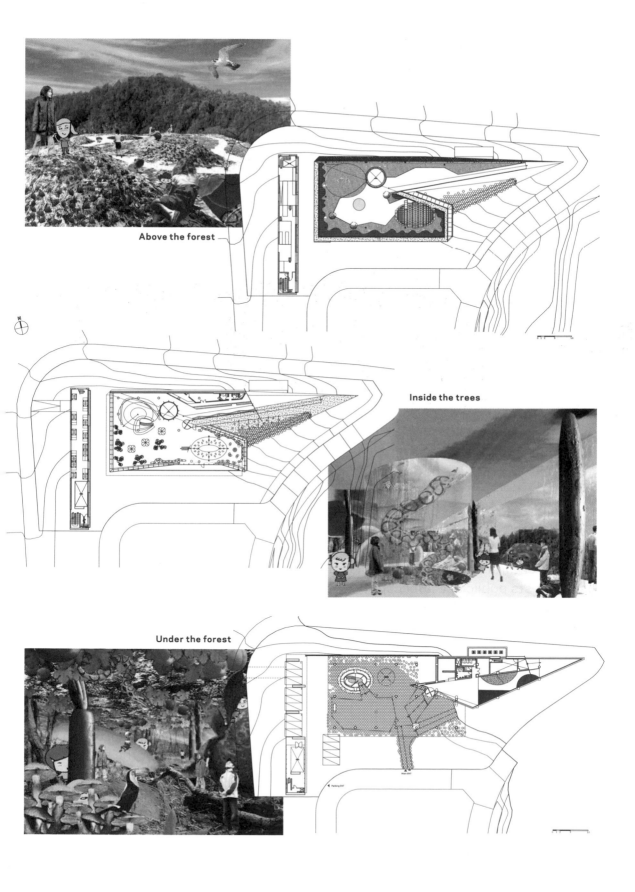

Above the forest

Inside the trees

Under the forest

Bapsang (meal table)' → Bapsang Sequence' In Korean 'Bapsang', every dish appears on the table at the same time; each person chooses the sequence and combination of the meal. In western meals, each course is designed with a specific combination of items and served in a specific sequence. The circulation strategy of this building allows

for both 'Bapsang' and sequential experiences of the space. You can go directly to a store and back out, or you can jump from area to area in any sequence, mixing shopping, playing and eating and small, medium and large scales. Areas can be experienced discretely, or short circuits can accommodate different user types.

Circulation System → The ability to jump between spaces, programs and scales or to stay within a zone is analogous to hypertext within a web document. You can either read through the text or click on the hypertext to jump directly to another space.

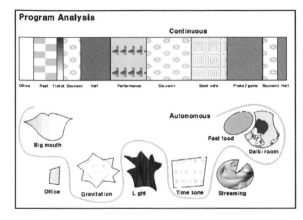

Program Analysis

Continuous

Office | Rest | Ticket | Souvenir | Hall | Performance | Souvenir | Book cafe | Photo / game | Souvenir | Hall

Autonomous

Big mouth

Fast food

Dalki room

Office | Gravitation | Light | Time zone | Streaming

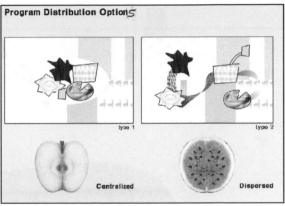

Program Distribution Options

type 1 | type 2

Centralized | Dispersed

'Play as organizational model' → Adults learn to categorize activities, which become "different" based on their categorization. For children there is initially no difference between play and work, play and learning, play and shopping... Play is everything and everything is play. It is through play that children begin to understand the world and society. Can a building reflect the most primary form of play with its smooth understanding of program and activity, creating a promiscuous zone with no boundaries between commercial, recreational and pedagogical activities?
Is it possible to mix adult definitions with this looser open structure? Can this coexist with a more traditional understanding of program areas and functions, to allow someone to enter, buy something, and leave?

Above the forest **1**

Inside the trees **2**

Under the forest **3**

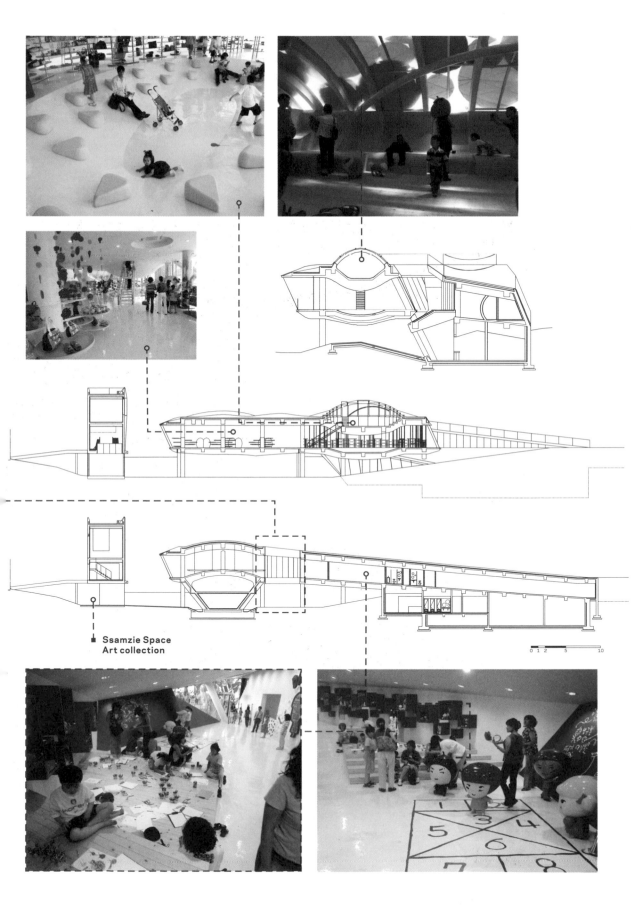

Ssamzie Space
Art collection

0 1 2   5   10

For the shady lower level, we wanted to create a unique synthetic outdoor environment where the ceiling suface is exploited to generate artificial climatic conditions. This ceiling is equipped with various light disks, fog machines, fans and heaters that provide effective conditioning of this space during the summer and winter months. The ground surface is composed of hexagonal tiles of two different materials – colored concrete and recycled rubber – and two different shapes for each material, flat tiles and bumps. Along with the artificial conditions generated by the ceiling surface, the varying ground surfaces seamlessly accomodate different activities such as play and rest areas.

Digital Scale → This building is about experimenting with 'scale'. Heyri city, the mountains, buildings, visitors, characters and natural and artificial objects are part of this playful collage of scales varying from micro to macro, from miniature to giant. Zones may have specific scale characteristics, but short circuit points allow immediate connection to areas of different scale. Generally, the lower level is occupied by over-scaled objects and giant creatures, the top open space with under-scaled objects and small creatures, and the middle level a mixture of the two.

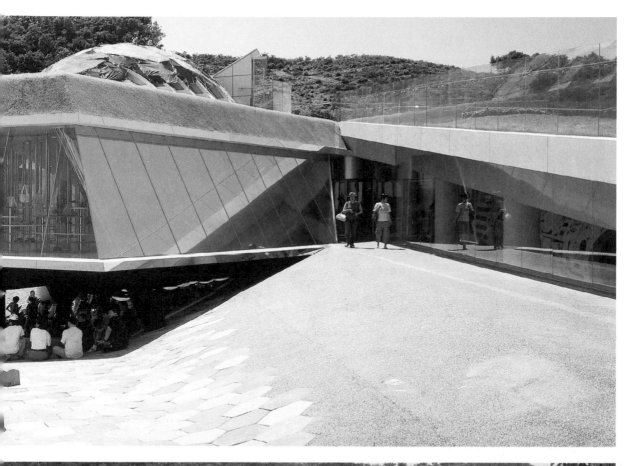

data

Dalki Theme Park - 'I Like Dalki' ➔ **Location:** H-69-1 Heyri Art Valley, South Korea. **Architecture:** Mass Studies (Minsuk Cho / principal, Kisu Park, Joungwon Lee, Soon Pyo Lee, Soonbok Choi) + Ga.A Architects (Moongyu Choi / principal, Jeonghui Kim, Kwangho Cha, Inchul Kang, Taekwon Yun, Bongki Song, Dae Gon Koh, Jeyong Kang) + Slade Architecture (James Slade / principal, Hayes Slade, Ilya Korolev, Francisco Pardo). **Interior:** Ga.A Architects (Moongyu Choi / principal, Jeonghui Kim, Jeyong Kang), Mass -Interior- Studies (Minsuk Cho / principal, Kisu Park, Soon Pyo Lee, Soonbok Choi, Hyunjung Kim, Byulnam Yoo), Hyungjoo Lee (artist collaborator), 44(Sasa)-44'sKick-Ass!!! ('Ddongchimi Tube' Mural). **Engineers:** Shin Structural Engineering (structure), Han On Engineering, Dong-Ho Engineering (M/E/P), Kyoung-In Engineering (civil) **Design period:** Jan. 2002 - Oct. 2002 **Construction period:** Jan. 2003 - June 2004. **Site area:** 3580 m². **Building area:** 470 m². **Photographs:** Yong Kwan Kim + Mass Studies (p. 184-185). **Model:** Design Seoul Model Co., Ltd. **General contractor:** Hanool Construction. **Client:** Ssamzie - Hokyun Chun, president. www.massstudies.com, www.gaa-arch.com, www.sladearch.com

between the Pyrenees and the sea...

verb

15°C

Villa Bio is a house created not to divide surfaces, separate one parcel from another, separate the house from the garden, divide it into rooms... instead, its organization is about continuity: an artificial landscape intimately connected to the earth, the sky and the woods that surround it. Conventional architectural elements like walls, ceilings and floors have disappeared, or are camouflaged as earth, trees and water. The linear trajectory of the house becomes a seamless extension of the nature that surrounds it.

Contemporary architecture is the platform for contemporary art and culture.
Dwelling is an existing platform that can be converted into art: the art of dwelling.
We conceive of this platform as a linear landscape of events, folded over on
the site to form an ascending spiral.

The slope of the adjacent woods extends into the house. From the street front to the back of the house, the floor rises 1.5 meters and another 1.5 meters from there to the upper front room. The same slope extends onto the roof in a continuous spiral movement.

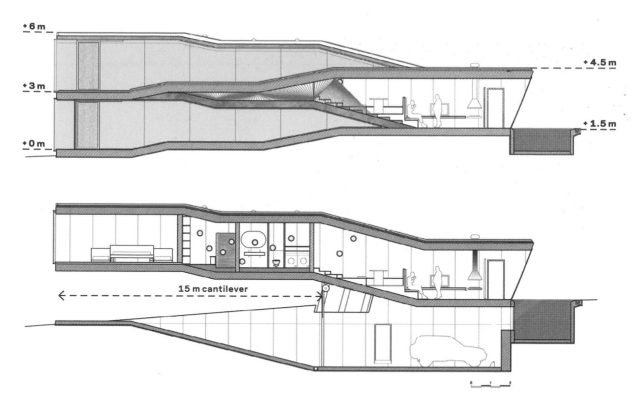

+ 6 m
+ 4.5 m
+ 3 m
+ 1.5 m
+ 0 m

← - - - - - 15 m cantilever - - - - - - →

0   1   2

The platform is a linear concrete structure with a constant C-shaped section, whose blind longitudinal façades act as beams to create a 15 meter-long projecting floor. The platform enters a liquid, mutant state, with a natural roof garden, an interior landscape of glass (block) with plotted digital renderings... A BIO architecture. (Patent pending.)

The planned swimming pool and the panoramic window will mirror each other.

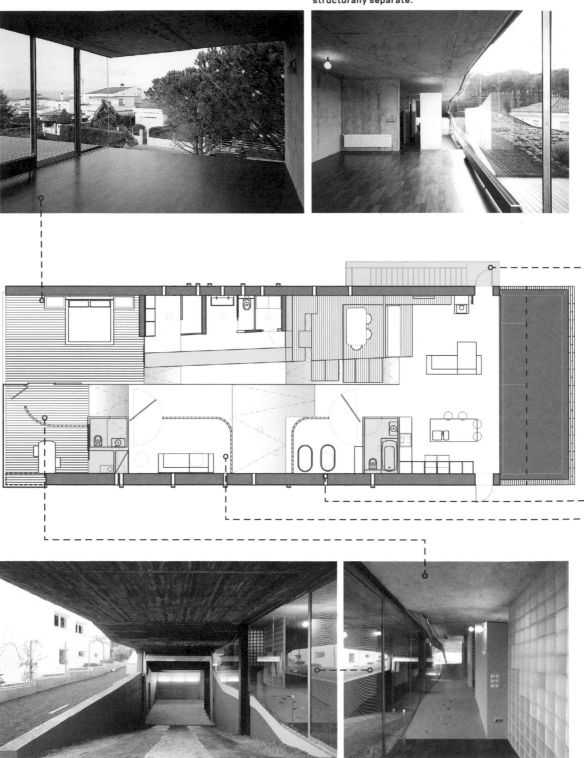

From the bedroom, looking toward the living room. The displaced concrete platforms are structurally separate.

Garage ramp. The front door is to the right.

Stairs connecting the garage
to the living room.

Kitchen (left),
living room (right)
and dining room
(three steps up).

There are no large windows
facing the neighbors, but
skylights and portholes
with thick glass fixtures
by Emiliana Design.

Artificial nature: pixelated
clouds in the glass block walls
that enclose the studio and
the children's bedrooms.

Panoramic window over the future swimming pool and
door to the basement garage. The light fixture (SIVRA,
by Iguzzini) is equipped with sensors that reproduce
the chromaticity of daylight.

Process

1 Creation of a 3D model of the topography to be constructed.
2 A Virilian landscape of events.

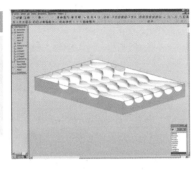

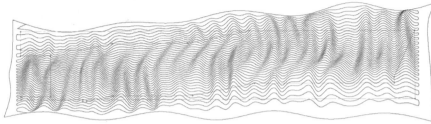

3 A CAD/CAM process with a triple-axis CNC mill is used to mold a single, non-standard image measuring 24 m x 3 m.

4 The mold is treated to act as the form-work for the north and south longitudinal façades.

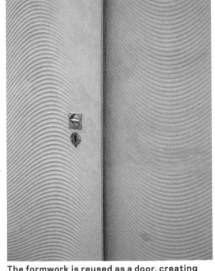

The formwork is reused as a door, creating the visual effect of a negative.

Façade
The concrete – a fluid material that solidifies – creates a "liquid" topography.

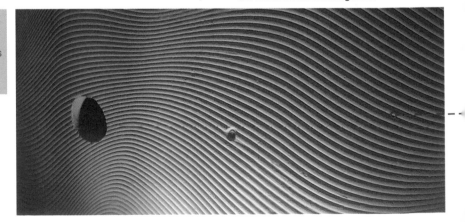

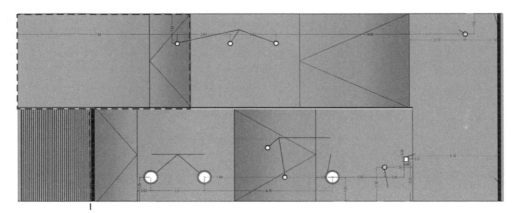

A typical house in this development occupies most of its small plot (800 m²), leaving very little space for a garden. In Villa Bio the garden moves on top of the house, displaced from its original condition.

From the garden, the house disappears, a continuation of the surrounding woods. Volcanic soil provides the base for an aromatic herb garden.

data

Villa Bio → Location: Llers, Girona. **Client:** The Fontecha family. **Architecture:** Cloud 9. **Main architect:** Enric Ruíz-Geli.
Engineer: Manel Raventós. **Interior design:** Manel Soler Caralps. **Clerk of works:** Arantza Garetaonandia. **Structure:**
Antonio Diosdado. **Services:** Joaquim Ribes Quintana. **Natural roof:** Jardines Burés. **Landscaping:** Joan Madorell.
Glass: Cricursa. **Appliances:** Emiliana Design Studio. **Metal detailing:** Alumínis Empordà. **Graphics:** Laia Jutglà. **Paving:**
Pavindus. **Moving surfaces:** Panalite. **Lighting:** Iguzzini. **Fixed surfaces:** Japlac. **Photographs:** Ramon Prat, Luis Ros.

Villa Nurbs
Enric Ruiz Geli - Cloud 9

verb

☀

21°C

Empuriabrava is a resort city of villas and weekend houses, an artificial environment where tropical landscape still appears as in a dream. The Nurbs House sits within this zone like a UFO. To build this house and to live in it are equal experiments, for both the architect and the client. Within the organic space of the house, acts of living like cooking and sleeping become spatial events, mediated by the material effects of concrete, ceramic tiles, fractals, water and air...

Process

1 Experiment with the accidents of breaking ice to create volumes of water.
2 Let natural materials define a landscape of pavilions.
3 Construct landscape as a platform for dwelling.
4 Measure and construct the landscape as a 3D topography.
5 The resolution of the topography will consist of contour lines every 45.15 and 5 cm.

FEM model used for the pre-dimensioning of the covering

Vertical displacements of the structural glass covering

Diagrams of efforts

Axial efforts in the concrete base according to local axes in each element. Green and blue correspond to compressed zones, orange to zones of almost null effort and red to tractioned zones.

6 The geometry is complex.
7 The reference will be a NURBS (Non-uniform Rational B-Spline) curve.
8 Seek a new materiality.
9 Optimize construction resources using CAD/ CAM processes.
10 Create this platform in a scalar fashion from the climate, the geography and the exterior landscape to the NURBS skin of the house.
11 Invited industrial designers work from the skin of the NURBS to the skin of the occupants, in pursuit of a cellular, chemical approximation to this materiality.
12 The design always involves the active participation of the client.
13 Definition of atmospheres inside the skin.
14 A skin with contents.
15 The skin is reactive and manages energies.
16 Democratize 'elite' architecture and bring 'high-tech' and 'opensoft' into housing.

It's happening: the work period is 2004-2006.

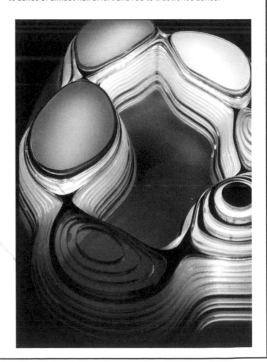

Initial concept → What would happen if we raised the house on two legs?
If we used the concrete volume of the swimming pool as a support for the house?
Where would the dwelling be?
Distributed in pavilions around the pool.

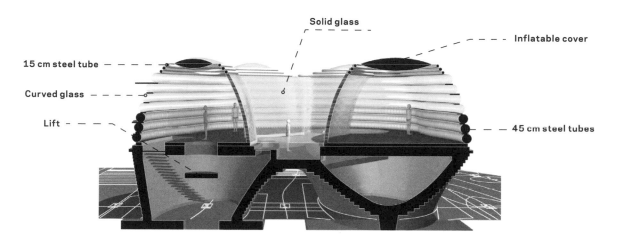

Solid glass

Inflatable cover

15 cm steel tube

Curved glass

Lift

45 cm steel tubes

Structural model → The house is situated by the sea on soft, moist ground.
The greater part of the structure is invisible: 50 foundation piles sunk to a depth
of 15 metres.

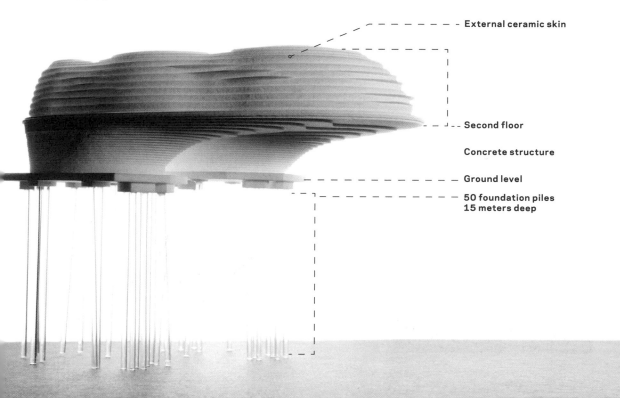

External ceramic skin

Second floor

Concrete structure

Ground level

50 foundation piles
15 meters deep

The formwork → Diorama is a company that specializes in carpentry for exhibitions and trade fairs. When our firm approached them, they had never produced formwork. The process of drawing every sheet of formwork required over three months of work, and Diorama cut all of the pieces with a machine saw in a single Saturday morning. All of the numbered pieces were delivered ready to assemble. The entire process cost 60,000 euros.

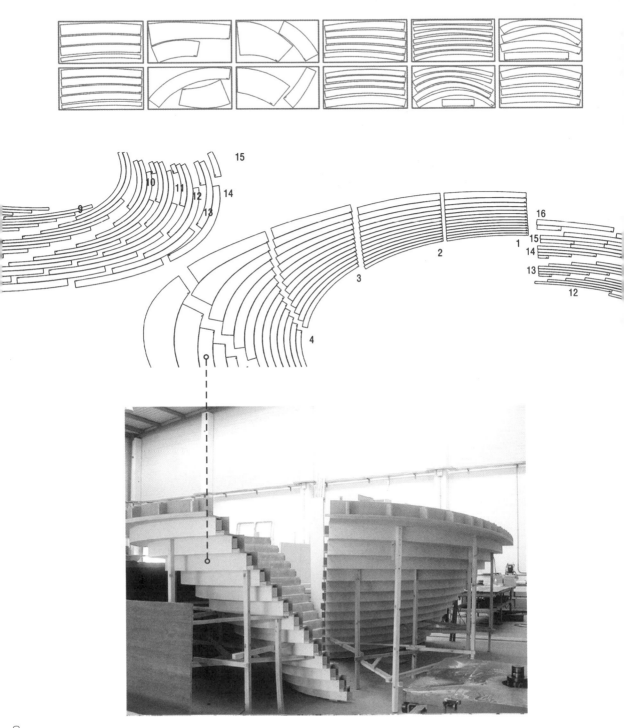

Thousands of temporary pillars support the projection of the concrete base, a roofed garden with an area of 150 m² that provides shelter from the strong sun.

The concrete contains an accelerating agent, a pigment that gives it its black color, a silicate powder that delays rejection by 20% and a very fine wool for greater strength.

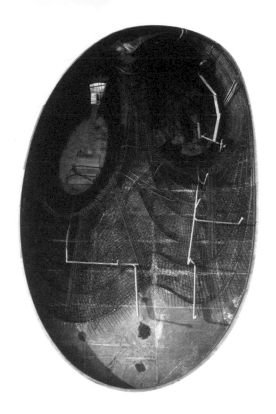

Aerial photographs of the concrete base under construction

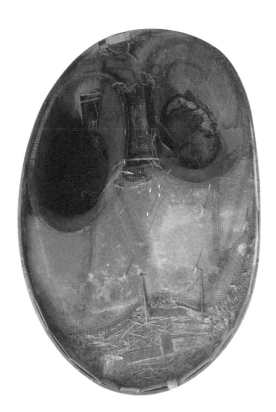
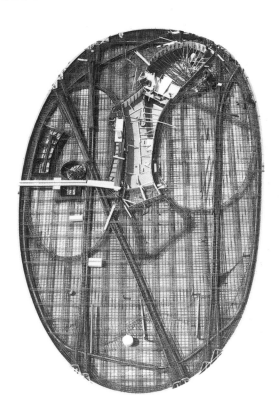

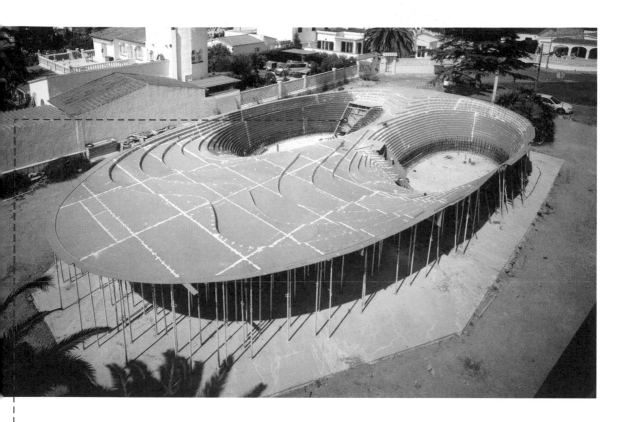

The entrance door is made of concrete infused with Porex and has two hydraulic motors, made by Ramon Presta, who mostly builds robots for exhibitions. The **lower part** of the villa consists of two spaces: a winter living room with a fireplace and a chill-out space that doubles as an office. Natural daylight enters from the pool above through a 9 m long sheet of glass, similar to those used in aquariums.

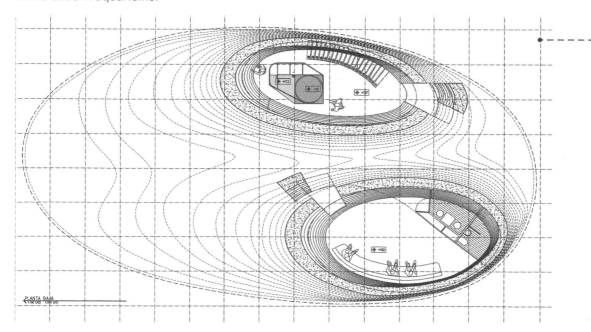

PLANTA BAJA

Skin → The skin is rough on the exterior but smooth on the inside. The interior skin of the upper level is made of 15 cm solid glass blocks with transparent 3 mm joints. We want the exterior skin to be of ceramic, like the roof of Gaudí's Casa Batlló. We have also invited Frederic Amat to create a fractal especially for the house. The roofs of the pavilions are of the same ETFE plastic used by Nicholas Grimshaw in the Eden Project. This is the first time that this material will be used in a house.

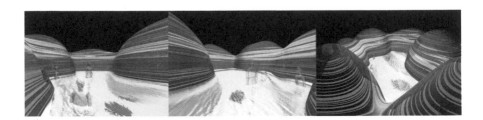

data

Villa Nurbs → Location: Empuriabrava, Girona. **Architecture:** Cloud 9. **Architect:** Enric Ruiz-Geli. **Associate architect:** Jordi Fernández. **Cloud 9 Team:** Alessandra Faticanti, Max Zinnecker, Susanne Bodach, André Brosel. **Structure:** Boma S.L.: Agusti Obiol, Guillem Baraut. **Clerk of works:** Dani Benito, Xavier Badia. **Design:** Emiliana Design Studio. **Environmental consultant:** Estudi Ramon Folch. **Special glass:** Cricursa. **Carpentry:** Diorama. **Concrete structure:** Construcciones Joan Fusté. **Metal structure:** Caldereria Delgado. **Projected concrete:** TES. **Landscaping:** Acycsa / Bures. **Services:** Electrica Vilalba. **Swimming pool:** Astral. **Metal detailing and locksmithing:** Industrias BEC, SA / Ramón Presta. **Photographs:** Ramon Prat, Luis Ros.

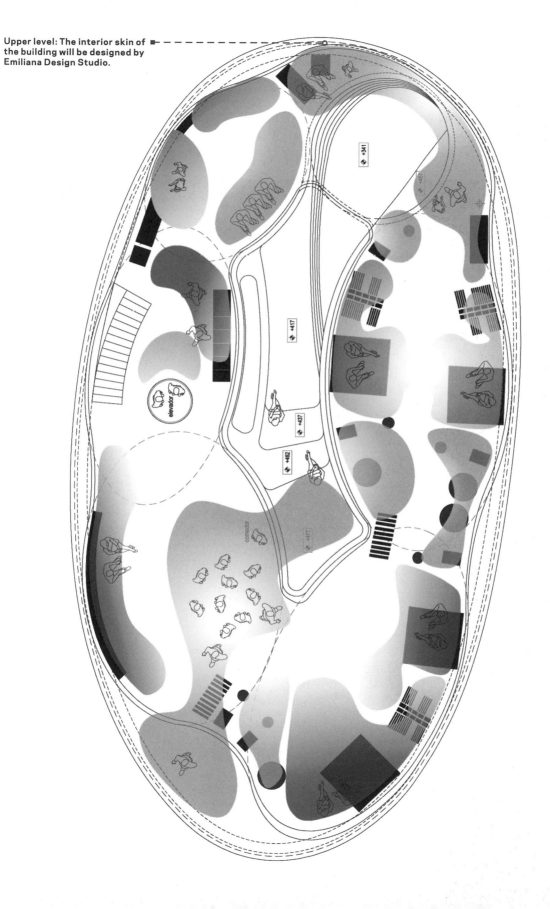

Upper level: The interior skin of
the building will be designed by
Emiliana Design Studio.

coming to Barcelona - "your house in a tree"

Hotel Habitat
Enric Ruiz Geli - Cloud 9

verb

27°C

The skin of this hotel pertains neither to the interior nor the exterior of the building: it mediates between the two, an ornamental wrap that defines a micro-climate around a dense and compact mass of rooms. A digital skin fabricated with LED's that incorporates real trees, collects energy through solar panels and transmits light and energy to the interior. The exterior becomes a hybrid laminate that situates the rooms of the hotel inside the canopy of a vertical forest.

The philosophies of architecture, commerce and marketing converge in pursuit of the idea of making a building like a **forest**: a building that learns from the energy behaviours found in nature, constructing a new nature for the urban façade of L'Hospitalet. Hotel Habitat is a **de-construction** of the hotel typology.

On the one hand, the building resolves the program of the hotel in an exposed concrete structure with glazed façades, a dense and highly functional organization that we call the **COMPACT**.

On the other, the image of the hotel by day and by night is combined with the sustainable philosophy of the developer to create a surface that we call **SKIN**, which envelops the COMPACT and resolves issues of views and exposure to sunlight coming from the south.

In the interstitial space between the COMPACT and the SKIN, a **microclimate** is created through the direct use of nature, with vertical planting (of the type of poplars that line the Gran Via de les Corts Catalanes) and the incorporation of natural greenery on both the façade and the roof.

The presence of nature acts like a lung for the neighborhood.

But there is another, "artificial" nature in the project: the SKIN is composed of a surface of stainless steel cables covered with 5,000 intelligent 'leaves' of LEDs and photovoltaic panels, a skin that both produces and consumes energy.

One the interior, the hotel creates a scenographic topography for the ground-floor restaurant with projectors and plasma screens, a technology that we call *animated wallpaper*. Together, the different projected images create the atmosphere of a hotel devoted to culture.

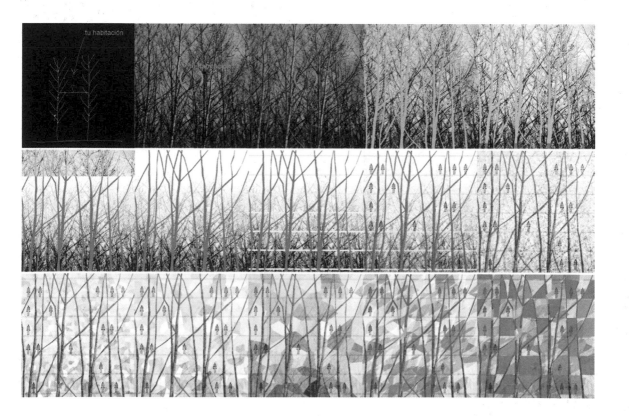

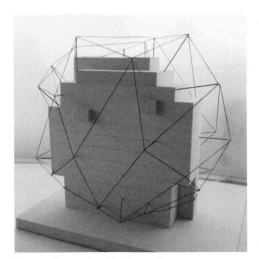

Skin studies made with wire and bent paper.

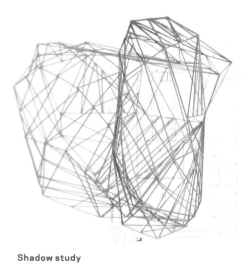

Shadow study

Skin parameters → A mesh of tension cables spaced at a distance of 40-50 cm.
Maximum projection over the street: 7 m
Artificial 'leaves': 5,000; resolution 9-16 per m²
Each leaf has a sensor, a photovoltaic plate, and an RGB LED (7 colors).

Summer

Winter

color-range		campo (C)	consumo (mA) 1 LED	potencia (V) R	G	B	total (W) sum (AxV)	tiempo (h)	consumo total (Wh) (= input placa 21.12.)
summer		7 (max)	10	1,9	3,2	3,8	0,089	12	1,068
		6	10		3,2	3,8	0,07	12	0,84
spring/ autumn		5	10	1,9		3,8	0,057	12	0,684
		4	10	1,9	3,2		0,051	12	0,612
		3	10			3,8	0,038	12	0,456
		2	10		3,2		0,032	12	0,384
winter		1 (min)	10	1,9			0,019	12	0,228

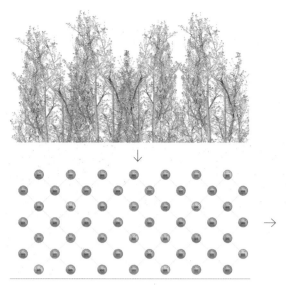

LED 'leaf' details
© patent in process

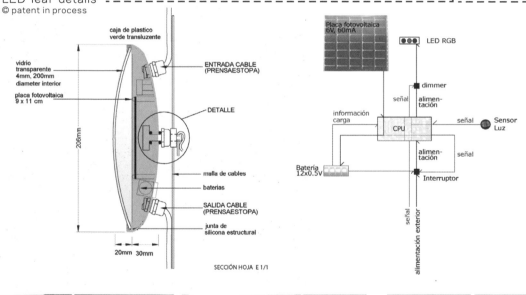

caja de plastico
verde transluzente

vidrio
transparente
4mm, 200mm
diameter interior

placa fotovoltaica
9 x 11 cm

206mm

ENTRADA CABLE
(PRENSAESTOPA)

DETALLE

malla de cables

baterias

SALIDA CABLE
(PRENSAESTOPA)

junta de
silicona estructural

20mm 30mm

SECCIÓN HOJA E 1/1

Placa fotovoltaica
6V, 60mA

LED RGB

dimmer

señal   alimen-
         tación

información
carga

CPU

señal   Sensor
         Luz

alimen-
tación

señal

Batería
12x0.5V

Interruptor

señal

alimentación exterior

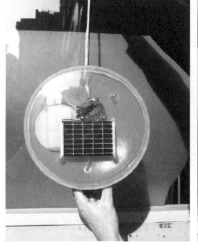

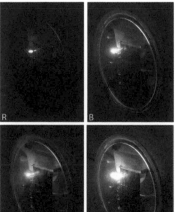

R   B

G   RGB

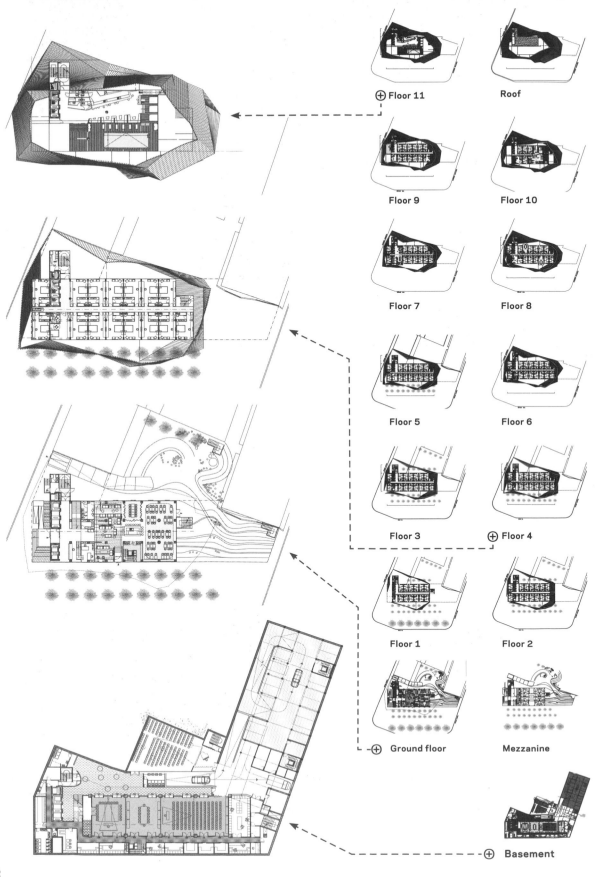

Floor 11

Roof

Floor 9

Floor 10

Floor 7

Floor 8

Floor 5

Floor 6

Floor 3

Floor 4

Floor 1

Floor 2

Ground floor

Mezzanine

Basement

Criteria

— Structure of exposed in-situ concrete with painted finish.
— Ease of access and optimum evacuation.
— Maximum number of rooms in relation to the area available for development.
— Expression and image through the LED skin.
— Identity and culture through an interior design based on the concept of a forest.
— Distinction based on quality of service, more than the size of the rooms.

The 4 x 3 m module of the façade generates an optimum division for rooms, each with a floor area of 18 m², as well as an optimum static system for the car park in the basement.
On upper portions of the façade, the modules define different types of terraces.

Built surface area above grade: 5,624 m²
Built surface area below grade: 3,964 m²
Total: 9,588 m²
Height: 40 m

Program

Ground Floor: Lobby, Lounge, Bar, Restaurant, Library, Zen Garden
Ground floor +1 to Ground Floor +11: 135 rooms
— 1 suite
— 2 junior suites
— 92 standard guest rooms
— 40 rooms on 3 VIP floors
Floors 6-9: Reception, breakfast room, meeting rooms, mediatheque on 3 VIP floors
Floor 10: Gym, sauna, massage, terrace with *haima* tent
Floor 11: Bar, terrace with pool
Basement:
— 650 m² of conference rooms:
— 350 m² of subdivisible rooms
— 150 m² auditorium and foyer
— 2 level car park (60 cars)

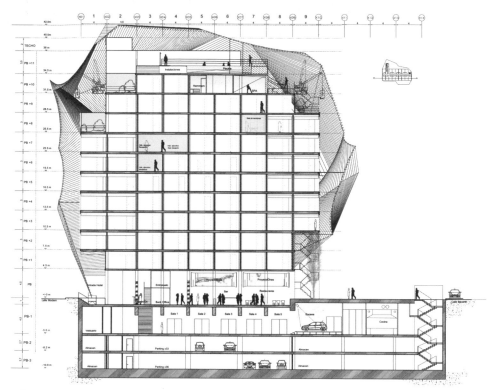

Longitudinal section

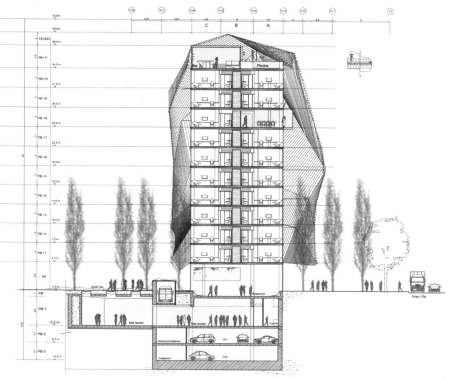

Transverse section

Each node of the facade captures daylight and glows at night: after sunset, the entire mass repeats the movement of light and shadow during the day. The design of this system will be carried out in collaboration with the artist Vito Acconci.

data **Habitat Hotel HR (New Hotel Restaurant Gran Via)** → **Location:** L'Hospitalet de Llobregat, Barcelona. **Architecture:** Cloud 9. **Client:** Grupo Inmobiliario Habitat. **Main architect:** Enric Ruiz-Geli. **Project architect:** Max Zinnecker. **Associate architects:** Ruy Ohtake and Vito Acconci Studio. **Collaborating architects Cloud 9:** Joscha Oberndörfer, Chiara Passa, Titusz Tarnai. **Structure:** Manuel Arguijo y asociados, SL. **Services:** PGI GRUP. **Models:** Guillermo Belluzo. **Graphics:** Laia Jutglà. **Photographs:** Luis Ros.

Black Treefrog
SPLITTERWERK

10°C

The existing building envelope of an old fire station is supplemented by a trellis and the addition of a new envelope, which is completely detached from the outer skin. The programs of daily life – kitchen niche, sleeping cove, bathing niche, etc. – are integrated into this in-between space. The new interior envelope is conceived of as a continuously active media surface with projections, enlarged picture screens or televisions that transform the spatial divisions into virtual phenomena.

To keep the envelope from entirely disappearing behind the foliage, the upper storeys were surrounded by an openwork walkway of galvanized metal that doubles as a continuous balcony. All the
windows opening onto the gallery have been enlarged to form doors. Advertising will eventually
cover the outside gallery, both to provide privacy and as a refinancing measure: a kind of "Times
Square in Bad Waltersdorf."

Ground floor

First floor

Second floor

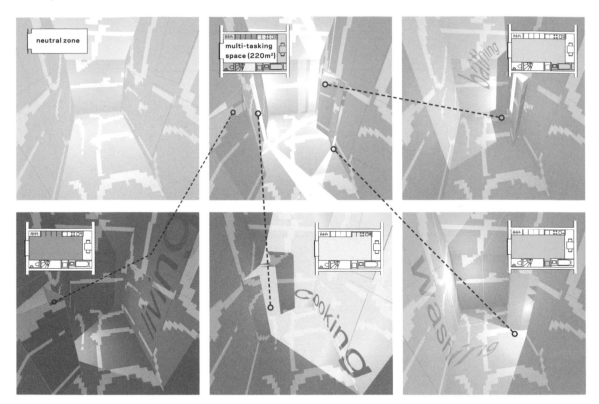

Radical densification of living → The apartments of the Black Treefrog are "multincident shells" informed by the functions and program requirements of dwelling and inhabitation. The floor area of each apartment is limited to 37 m², of which 22 m² becomes a functionally neutral core. The remaining 15 m² are filled with specific domestic functions, each individually activated and separately extending into the neutral zone. In this way it is possible to arrange baths, kitchens, dining spaces and bedrooms that each measure 22 m². Thus the space is ten times 22 m² – the equivalent of a 220 m² apartment.

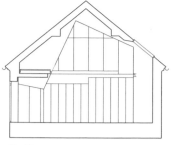

Section

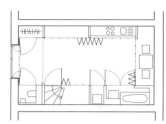

Ground floor

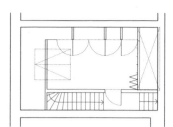

First floor

 Springy floor of metal mesh: the bed is stored in the wall until ready for use and slides out on metal tracks.

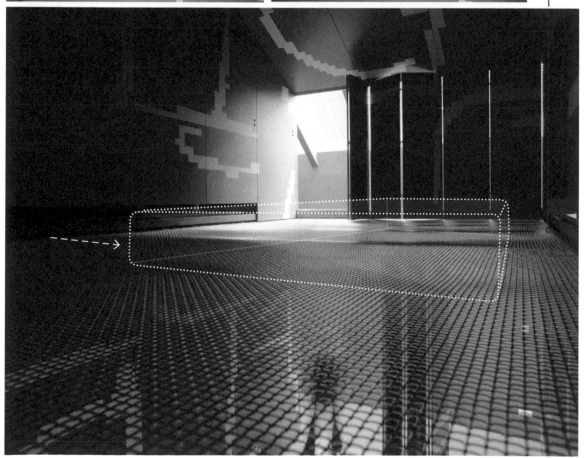

data

Black Treefrog → Location: Bad Waltersdorf, Austria. **Design:** SPLITTERWERK. **Architects and artists:** Splitterwerk. **Project team:** Mark Blaschitz, Hannes Freiszmuth, Johann Grabner, Edith Hemmrich, Bernhard Kargl, Antje Neitsch, Gernot Ritter, Josef Roschitz, Andreas Stampfer. **Project management:** Barnds United, Grabner & Partner Ziviltechniker KEG für Architektur. **Building contractor:** Bau-Pilz BaugesmbH. **Video and video stills:** Nikolaos Zachariadis, Markus Max Nagler. **Client:** Franz and Gertrude Brugner. **Construction:** Bau-Pilz, Cserni Wohnen, Bscheider, Heco, Holz Bau Weiz. Site area: 1214 m². **Floor area:** 620m². **Number of floors:** 3. Project date: 10/1998. Construction: 2/2003- 6/2004. **Net building costs:** 650.000 €. **Photographs:** Paul Ott, Graz

The surface of the main stairway in the Black Treefrog references local grapevines, which, in addition to the wooden trellis, transforms the entire exterior into a landscape. The floors, walls, ceilings and steps of the staircase are treated as similar formal elements and are covered with a dense patterning of differently sized and detailed vine leaves. The informed surfaces influence the three-dimensional effect of the whole. The stair construction is seen less as a form in space and more as a programmatic division of the entry, splitting access into two zones: one for the ground floor and another for the first story. The absence of closed risers creates a visual connection between these physically and functionally divided zones as the surface patterns blur the distinction between foreground and background. The constructive and functional parts of the main stair are overlaid with an "informed" surface: a pattern of grape leaves that simultaneously breaks down lines and edges such that the geometry of the ensemble begins to dissolve. The space transforms into a sphere.

See page 256

Tomihiro Museum
aat+ Makoto Yokomizo

verb

More bubble-atmospheres. Start with the most basic figure – a circle – proliferate and combine. An architecture developed from the smallest spatial unit, the room and its continuity with other rooms. The resulting aggregate has no entirety: the square of the perimeter is defined by intersection with the various bubbles, a transparent section through a diverse collection of environmental specimens. On the interior, visitors experience a continuous sequence of distinct atmospheres, each with its own color, materials, temperature, light, functions and views. The circles of the interior have no directionality: like walking through the forest, we can only look for a pleasant clearing in which to rest.

7°C

A small museum dedicated to an artist → The artist Tomihiro Hoshino was born in the small village of Azuma in 1946, and became a junior high school physical education teacher. In 1970 he suffered a severe accident and was confined to a wheelchair. No longer able to use his arms and hands, Tomihiro began to draw and write with his mouth during his recovery period in the hospital. In 1991, officials in Azuma converted a pre-existing social facility into a museum to exhibit Tomihiro's watercolors. Surprisingly, in the ten years since its opening, over 4 million visitors have come to this small museum in Azuma, a village of only 3,500 residents. The original museum facility lacked the necessary infrastructure to accommodate so many visitors, and in 2002, aat + Makoto Yokomizo won the competition for a new museum.

Concept / Makoto Yokomizo

Non-white cubes → When I first encountered the works of Tomihiro Hoshino, I found that every element of his natural world is perceived differently due to his character and condition. While designing this museum for his works, I thought it would be non-sense to make homogenous and neutral white cubes. Instead, we outlined four basic design concepts: non-centrality, non-totality, relativity and heterogeneity.

Non-centrality We no longer live in a world of hierarchy, but rather in a network.
Non-totality There is no single correct strategy in planning. Our proposal is only one possible outcome for accommodating the program.
Relativity To create a simple format for the plan, we simply drew circles with the appropriate square footage for each program, assembling them to form a museum.
Heterogeneity. The sensation of being in a natural forest. There is light, dark-ness, silence, cheer, warmth, coolness and wind; these differences help direct the movement of visitors to the museum. We tried to foster co-existence and diversity, accepting the reality of their complexities.

Circle planning → The circle has many special characteristics: it is a strong form, generated solely by a center point and a radius. It is structurally strong and, when its surface is kept rigid, a very thin cylinder can be extruded. The circle is primitive, allowing it to be easily understood by all the non-architects who participated in the planning. The combination and aggregation of circles propagates further charac-teristics. Circles are both absolute and relative, flexible and strong, abstract and concrete, capable of accepting various programmatic elements. Our hope was to push them beyond either indigenous locality or the abstraction of modern architec-ture. A total of 2,700m² of triangular spaces between the circular program spaces adds a sense of porosity to the structure, where a bit of "outside" appears "inside." Carefully selected plant species grow freely in these in-between spaces, filling the building with life.

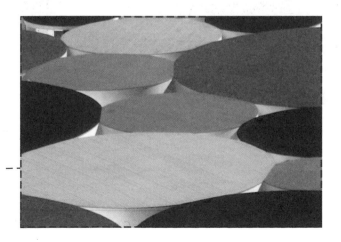

Square → Rather than determining the outline of the building according to the shape of the site, we cut this group of circular spaces into a square to maintain the clear idea of a generic, abstract design. The proposal thus creates a universal system that can accept a completely different program, or a completely different site. Le Corbusier's series of "infinite growth" museums (like the Centre d'art Contemporain from 1931) and Mies's New National Gallery (1968) are designed as abstract buildings floating on pilotis, set down carefully on the ground but detached from it. In Tomihiro's museum, we wanted a similar freedom from the specificity of the site, an abstraction of contemporary architecture achieved by designing it as a square.

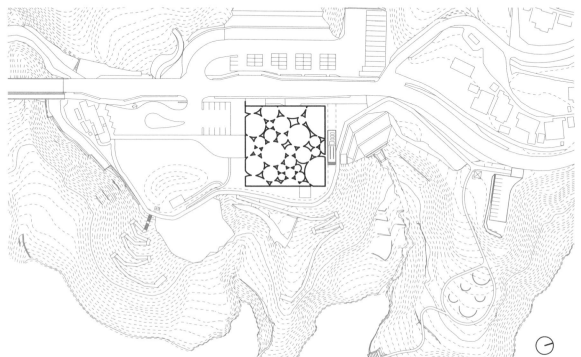

Self-optimization → During the competition, Mitsuhiro Kanada of Ove Arup & Partners in Japan joined the project. I had already developed the idea of using a gathering of circles and showed him a photo of soap bubbles to illustrate my idea. When he saw the photo, he said "the bubbles seek self-optimization." The idea of making a building that optimizes itself in hardware and software is very attractive. These terms are from the computer industry, but I understand them as a practice by which codes are replaced and continually improved depending on its processing method and evolution. These systems are complicated in the micro sense, but very simple in the macro sense, much like how a sunflower follows the sun. We have tried to translate this process into architecture, fashioning each environment to best suit people's activities and needs. Of course, since the building itself doesn't move, we varied the spaces instead. During the design phase, the museum curators also helped us by cutting circular bits of paper and offering variations for the arrangement of spaces. In the final

Self-optimization of bubbles: Two bubbles sandwiched between glass. When the bubbles touch each other, they automatically seek the most stable distance and position.

construction stage , Tomihiro Hoshino expressed his satisfaction with the project, saying, "We are made of round cells and the earth is also round. Thus, this building would be very natural."

A World with Variation → We hoped to make the building like a natural forest: a place of varied spaces with different characteristics of light, dark, silence, cheerfulness, warmth and cool. Visitors have both a feeling of shelter and a sense of curiosity and expectancy as they pass through the different circular spaces, waiting to see what comes next. Each circle has a different size and environment depending on its needs. Here, environments are determined by intensity of light, color, acoustic characteristics, temperature, humidity, acid-alkaline balance, and quantity of volatile organic material. Other factors are more difficult to quantify numerically, like openness, closure, or comfort. The demands of each room are solved locally, with different wall, ceiling and floor finishes in each case. Lighting techniques and air-conditioning systems are also unique to each room. The exhibition spaces are lightcontrolled with constant temperature and humidity levels and are painted in matte tones to accommodate works sensitive to light and humidity, while rooms with exterior views are bright, open and finished with glossy materials to amplify their qualities.
The arrangement of the circular spaces is determined by fixing the relationship between each space, much like working out a puzzle. There are no general restrictions, nor is there a single absolute solution. The circular spaces each have their own function and are combined according to their necessary position relative to the whole. From a structural point of view, this bundle of distinctly sized cylinders is quite solid. Each cylinder is attached to the surrounding cylinders, and, in unison, the collection of cylinders is highly resistant to earthquakes and wind stresses.

The necessary programs and their sequence, with supporting rooms.

Without breaking the sequence, the programs are shifted to touch each other.

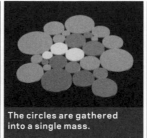

The circles are gathered into a single mass.

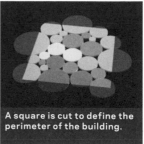

A square is cut to define the perimeter of the building.

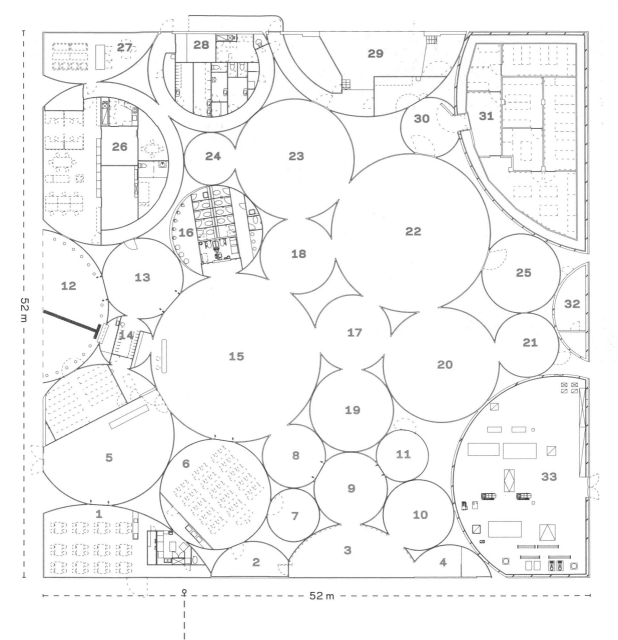

This museum contains 33 circles of rooms.
Each room has a different function – exhibition
hall, screening room, shop, cafe – and is made
of different materials or colors.

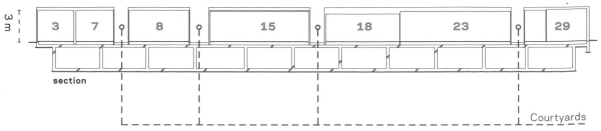

section

Courtyards

Randomness and Sequentiality → The works of Tomihiro Hoshino are all small. There is not much difficulty in hanging them on a curved wall, which we confirmed with a full-scale mock-up. A round exhibition space is completely different from a rectilinear one. In a square room, the importance of position varies with proximity to the corner and the directionality of the walls. Upon entering a square room, the front wall usually contains the featured or most important work in the space. In a round room, this spatial layout is impossible, since the wall simply continues without hierarchy. All surfaces are equivalent, allowing every work to be treated in the same way. Curators can then arrange works linearly, like a film montage.

1_Cafe
2_Back garden
3_Lounge
4_Exit
5_Shop
6_Lecture room
7_Storage
8_Information
9_Lithograph, silkscreen works
10_Information
11_Vestibule 3
12_Entrance
13_Vestibule 1

14_Ticket counter, locker room, cloak room
15_Lobby
16_Lavatory
17_Entrance to the exhibition rooms
18_Exit from the exhibition rooms
19_Exhibition hall 1
20_Exhibition hall 2
21_Small exhibition room 1
22_Exhibition hall 3

23_Exhibition hall 4
24_Small exhibition room 2
25_Supply room
26_Office, storage room
27_Director's room
28_Employee area
29_Carry-in space
30_Anterior room for storage
31_Storage for works
32_Machine room 2
33_Machine room 1

The round exhibition space → The sequential continuity of the space is interrupted only by the passage from one cylinder to another. However, there is no need to move in a linear sequence: visitors can pass from the first to the fourth exhibition room or skip into any other adjacent space. Thus the spaces become very much like the "random access sequential" files found in computers. This randomness and sequentiality can accommodate all types of visitors, from the relaxed individual to tourist groups with strict time schedules.

The cafe is at the southeast corner of the building, with two glass façades. The east façade, facing the lake, is made of chemically treated leaves sandwiched between glass, and the glass on the south façade is finished with a sandblasted dot pattern.

Looking towards the kitchen from the south window

1

Cafe (Wood)

The shadow of the small round windows that look onto the interior patios.

Material finish test for south façade glass

The floor is finished with 12mm-thick painted walnut panels. The walls and ceiling are finished with fireproof natural wooden panels on plaster board with bonded fiberglass fabric.

A paper window, made with traditional Japanese artesanal techiques in a local factory. In the process of layering and drying, water is dripped on the paper to produce a special pattern for the window, reminiscent of falling snow.

2

Paper window with water drop pattern

Back garden (Paper)

Traditional Japanese paper factory

The walls, floor and ceiling of the lounge are finished in stainless steel mirror, reflecting views of the mountains and the lake, the patios between the circles, curtains and visitors. The curtains, designed by NUNO, have a layer of broken holes, which has an effect similar to the paper window in room 2.

Lounge (Mirror)

3

Graphic pattern of the window

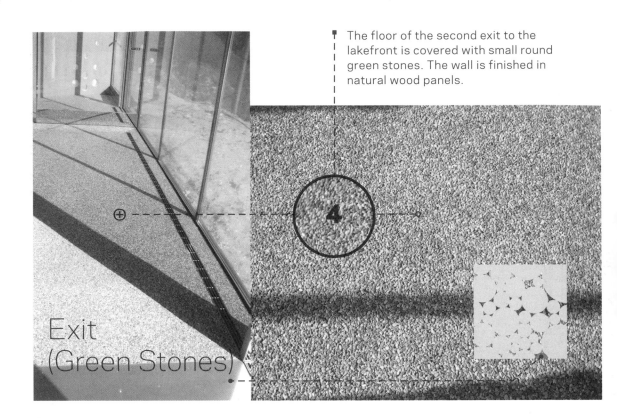

The floor of the second exit to the lakefront is covered with small round green stones. The wall is finished in natural wood panels.

4

Exit
(Green Stones)

The wall of the shop is made of foamed aluminum to absorb noise.

5

Shop
(Aluminum)

Information (Wood)

8

The information room is finished in natural wood panels, with fluorescent tube lamps arranged randomly on the ceiling.

Lithograph and silkscreen works (Blue glass)

The floor of the room is covered with bits of blue glass

9

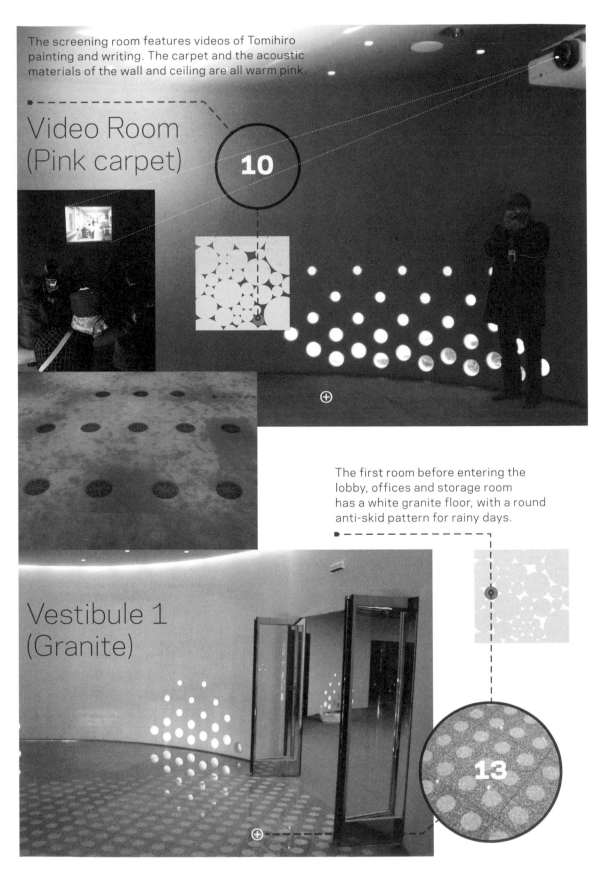

The screening room features videos of Tomihiro painting and writing. The carpet and the acoustic materials of the wall and ceiling are all warm pink.

Video Room
(Pink carpet)

10

The first room before entering the lobby, offices and storage room has a white granite floor, with a round anti-skid pattern for rainy days.

Vestibule 1
(Granite)

13

The window of the office is covered by sheets printed with a graduated pixel pattern to reduce direct sunlight.

Office (Pixel Glass)

The museum director's room is ivory in color. The west window is made of laminated glass with very thin natural wood sheets, transmitting natural light through the wood pattern. The floor is finished in a thick, soft carpet.

Director's Room (Translucent Wobd)

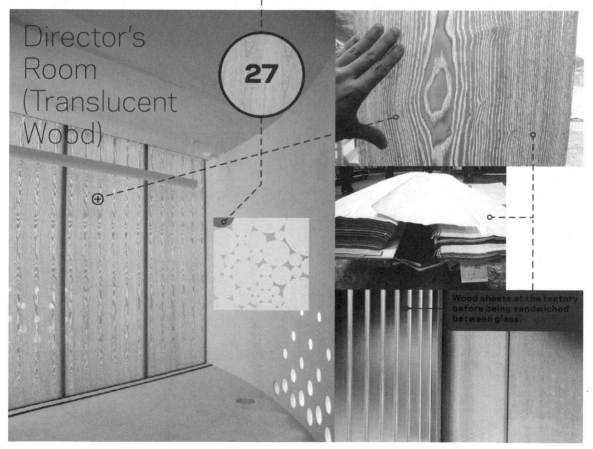

Wood sheets at the factory before being sandwiched between glass.

Lobby

Tomihiro visits the building site towards the end of construction.

The lobby is the node that connects all the functions of the museum, joining 8 rooms directly: ticket counter, exhibition rooms, shop, lecture room, lounge...
The floor is made of artificial wood, the wall is finished in acrylic emulsion paint on plaster board with fiberglass, and the ceiling is covered with rock wool acoustic board and fluorescent lights.

15

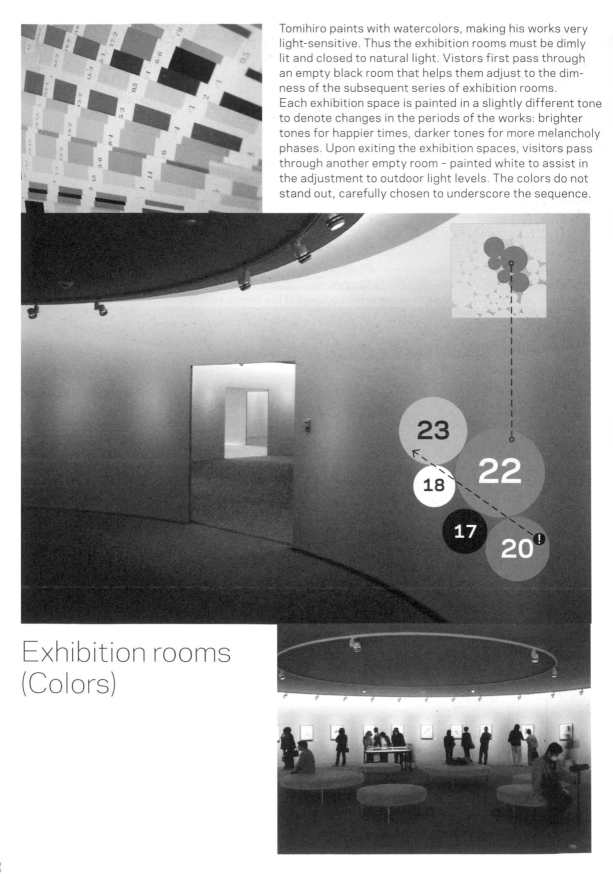

Tomihiro paints with watercolors, making his works very light-sensitive. Thus the exhibition rooms must be dimly lit and closed to natural light. Vistors first pass through an empty black room that helps them adjust to the dimness of the subsequent series of exhibition rooms. Each exhibition space is painted in a slightly different tone to denote changes in the periods of the works: brighter tones for happier times, darker tones for more melancholy phases. Upon exiting the exhibition spaces, visitors pass through another empty room – painted white to assist in the adjustment to outdoor light levels. The colors do not stand out, carefully chosen to underscore the sequence.

Exhibition rooms (Colors)

↗ A black room for visitors' eyes to adjust to the darkness of the coming exhibition rooms.

A white room after the exhibition halls to adjust to natural light. ↙

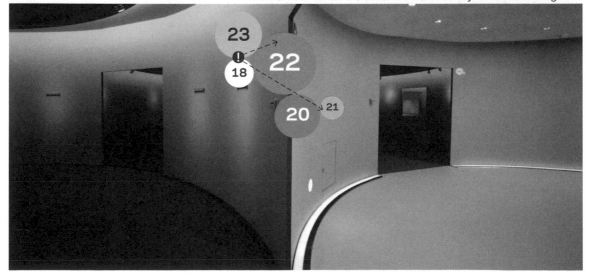

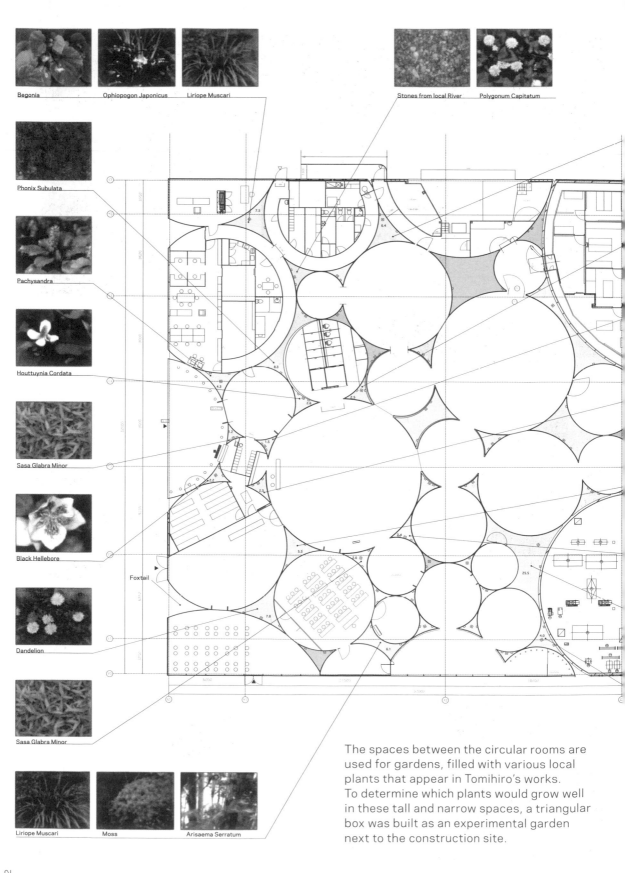

Begonia

Ophiopogon Japonicus

Liriope Muscari

Stones from local River

Polygonum Capitatum

Phonix Subulata

Pachysandra

Houttuynia Cordata

Sasa Glabra Minor

Black Hellebore

Foxtail

Dandelion

Sasa Glabra Minor

Liriope Muscari

Moss

Arisaema Serratum

The spaces between the circular rooms are used for gardens, filled with various local plants that appear in Tomihiro's works. To determine which plants would grow well in these tall and narrow spaces, a triangular box was built as an experimental garden next to the construction site.

Trial Garden for 7

Hakonechola Macra

Iris Gracilipes

Strawberry Geranium

Liriope Muscari

Ophiogogon Japonicus

The various types of gardens contain plants, mortar or stone. The courtyards can be seen through small circular windows, and each garden has small crawl entrance for maintainance.

Courtyards between the circles

Experimental garden

Phonix Subulata, Violet, Matteuccia Struthiopteris, Fern, Patasites Japonicus, Lily of Valley, Tricyrtis Hirta, Hosta Sieboldiana, Calanthe, Cymbidium Goeringii, Farfugium Japonicum, Japanese Andromeda, Lycoris Radiata, Wild Chryssanthemum, Bergenia Stracheyi, Enkianthus Perulatus, Gentian, Madagascar Periwinkle, Nasturtium, Stones

Moss   Liriope Muscari

Local plants painted by Tomihiro

Stones from local river and Ophiopogon Japonicus

Mortar finish

Stainless mirror panel   Aluminum panel   Marble   Wood sandwiched between glass

On the exterior, each section of the façade is made of different materials depending on the functions behind them and their relation to the outside. Some are open, some are closed; some are translucent, others perforated.

Sandblasted glass   Channel glass   Glass with printed pixel pattern

data

Tomihiro Museum, Azuma, Japan → **Location**: Azuma, Gumma Prefecture, Japan. **Client**: Azuma village. **Design**: aat+ Makoto Yokomizo, architects inc. **Structure**: Mitsuhiro Kanada, Arup Japan. **Construction period**: September 2004 - April 2004. **Plot area**: 18,573.4 m². **Floor area**: 2,463.5 m². **Number of floors**: 1. **Structure**: Steel (partially in reinforced concrete). **Dimensions**: 52 x 52 m, maximum height 3.50m. **Photographs**: Ramon Prat, Verb, aat+ Makoto Yokomizo, Kazuko Osawa. **www.aatplus.com**

Stainless mirror panel

Sandblasted glass

Leaves sandwiched between glass

verb

A conspicuous feature of many of the projects in this issue (you may have noticed) is a new merging of architecture and ecology. By now we are accustomed to buildings conceived as fields or grounds, undulating landscapes that mimic natural environments. What is more unexpected is the real integration of natural matters and processes into architecture, an aggressive removal of the operative distinction between the natural and the artificial. Both participate in equal measures; it no longer matters where one ends and the other begins. This shift reshapes the everyday practice of architecture: buildings become hybrid ecologies, requiring new criteria for judging the true capacities of the "natural" and the "man-made." The next issue of Verb looks more closely at architecture's "new natures", a survey of the territories we increasingly occupy in the age of real artificiality.

Patterned glass

Granite

verb

Verb Conditioning is the fourth volume of Actar's boogazine.
It was edited by Albert Ferré, Irene Hwang, Michael Kubo, Ramon Prat, Tomoko Sakamoto and Anna Tetas, with the participation of Jaime Salazar, graphic design by David Lorente and Reinhard Steger, and the collaboration of everyone here at Actar. Printed by Ingoprint and distributed by our in-house representatives.

Our thanks to all authors whose generous contribution of ideas and materials has made this issue possible. In addition, this publication has relied on the invaluable collaboration of Makoto Wada of att+, Takeyoshi Matsuda of ABRF, Kenichi Matsuzawa of FOA, Giuseppe Blengini, Consuelo Ciavarella and Laura Luccioli of Massimilano Fuksas Arch., Galin Ersinija of Fondazione Fiera Milano, William McGee, Chris Leary and Jean Brown of The Stubbins Associates, Melissa Vaughn of the Harvard Graduate School of Design, Stefano Casciani, Gruen Associates, Hertha Hurnaus, Christian Oliver, Alex Wall, Peter Waugh, Sarah Whiting and Ron Witte.

Contact info
ACTAR
Roca i Batlle 2
E-08023 Barcelona
www.actar.es
phone +34 93 418 77 59
fax: + 34 93 418 67 07
verb@actar-mail.com

Distribution
ACTAR D
office@actar-d.com
phone: +34 93 417 49 93
fax: +34 93 418 67 07

ISBN: 84-95951-86-X
DL B-33695-05

**Printed and bound
in the European Union**